RECLAIM YOUR LIFE

3/12

to Dearest Jan & Charlie

thankyou for your support!

Always honor yourself

fondly.

Carole

RECLAIM YOUR LIFE

You and the Alcoholic/Addict

CAROLE BENNETT, MA

Sea Hill Press
Santa Barbara

Reclaim Your Life is a work of nonfiction.
Although the people and their stories are real and all events depicted herein
did occur, names and other minor details have been changed to protect privacy.

Produced by
Sea Hill Press, Inc.
Santa Barbara, California
www. seahillpress.com
Production Manager: Greg Sharp
Editor: Cynthia Sharp
Design & Layout: Judy Petry

Published 2010
ISBN 978-0-615-33104-1

Printed in the United States of America

This book is dedicated to the millions of families and friends who painfully love an alcoholic/addict.

A percentage of the proceeds of this book will be donated to recovery program scholarships.

Acknowledgments

Special thanks to the following professionals who helped me with my journey of seeing this dream become a reality:

Valerie and Russell Bishop, Cyndi and Greg Sharp, Andrea Barzvi, Jaimee Garbacik, Amy Kovarick, Tass Jones photography, Ellen McKenzie, Marc Jaffe, Nancy Keatinge, Natalie Sims, Liz Camfiord, Lorrie Thomas, Raymond Chandler, ESQ., Marcy Luikart, Deborah Gerken, David Brownfield, Andrea Ballas of CBS Publicity, Alana B. Elias Kornfeld of *The Huffington Post*, Claire R. of Al-Anon Family Group Headquarters Inc., Robert J. Lindsey, President and CEO of The National Council on Alcoholism and Drug Dependence Inc. (NCADD), the staff and beneficiaries of The Salvation Army Adult Rehabilitation Center (ARC), Carpinteria, California, the staff and clients of Project Recovery/The Council of Alcoholism and Drug Abuse (CADA), Santa Barbara, California.

Boatloads of thanks to my wonderful clients who over the years shared with me their sorrows and triumphs and have graciously allowed me to use their experiences in this book.

No acknowledgment would be complete without including one's family for their continued love and support. Thank you to Michael Pfeil, Joan and Bill Vogel, Callie and Samantha Bennett, Stephanie Beeman, Gail Rose Kane, Sarah Cavallaro and Vinny.

Last but not least, thanks to the Montecito Lower Village Starbucks, for on a daily basis extending to me an inviting place to write this book.

CONTENTS

PREFACE

I believe that ideas are born not only out of dreams, but out of necessity. How did we ever get along without zippers, Velcro, or rolling suitcases? We made do until someone felt that there must be a better alternative, something more convenient or less back breaking. Sometimes these "revolutionary" changes happen overnight; other times they take years to come to fruition.

I wouldn't begin to believe that this book is as awe inspiring or important as any of the above, but if a guide like this had been available to me years ago, I might not have spent so many sleepless, fearful, and sad nights wondering what I should or should not have done regarding my loved ones' substance abuse issues. For that reason, I hope this book can be of help and perhaps serve as a lifeline for you to navigate through the pain and suffering of loving an alcoholic / addict.

My family of origin was not much of a drinking clan. My mother had one, maybe two, drinks in the evening, and my father enjoyed a dry martini most nights. Neither of my siblings drank, and the occasional bottle of festival wine was sanctioned more to the drain than to our little cups. I can't recall our family ever opening a bottle of wine at dinner.

My substance-free world changed when, unbeknownst to me, I married an alcoholic. At first I justified his anger and mercurial behavior to the stress of his job. When things on his creative front were going well, the atmosphere was calm in our home. However, those times got fewer and farther between, and the days started clocking in with more tension and anxiety. As if his drinking was not enough to dismember our family unity, his son had come to live with us and was supporting a full-blown addiction to heroin.

We had adopted two beautiful little girls, and our youngest daughter was starting to show signs of addictive behavior from an early age. My family was being torn apart before my very eyes, and I was lost in grief, anguish, frustration, fear, and a black hole out of which I had no idea how to crawl. I had no clue how to help them or how to help myself.

After years of enduring this rollercoaster ride, my husband finally started attending a Twelve Step recovery program. His son entered a residential program, and our daughter attended special schools to help her with her addictions.

Sadly, I came to realize that though I didn't like him as an alcoholic, I didn't like his sobriety either. Even though he wasn't drinking any longer, he became easily annoyed and snapped at the slightest provocation. I found myself getting into more arguments with him than ever, and I came to understand that my husband was probably resentful and blaming me for strongly requesting that he stop his love affair with his bottle of "Early Times."

Through the years of addiction that permeated my family, I attended Al-Anon Twelve Step recovery meetings, augmented those with seeing a counselor, and even made a few visits to my religious advisor, yet no one could help me with the specifics of my plight. I didn't know how to act or what to say to improve our marriage or how to deal with our children's addiction issues. My husband's and my communication was tense, and little was accomplished; my boundaries were pitiful, and I was becoming an expert on rescuing and enabling.

Eventually the pressure became too much for me; my life felt unmanageable. My husband and I went our separate ways, and our daughter split her time between households when not in school.

After my divorce, I needed a major personal, emotional, and psychological change. I moved from Los Angeles to Santa Barbara, where I returned to school to pursue a Masters in Clinical Psychology. I intended to become a midlife-crisis counselor, but as fate would have it, I did my graduate hours at The Salvation Army Adult Rehabilitation Center, a six-month, male-population, residential/work-based program for recovering alcoholics and addicts. It seemed that I was completing the substance abuse education that had eluded me for years. At the Center, I counseled twenty clients a week about their fears, uncertainties, hopes, and dreams. We discussed their love affairs with their drug of choice, their consequences, relapses, and desires for recovery. I spent hours talking to the families about their loved ones' addictions and how they could participate in their recovery without controlling them or compromising their own lives.

I started to see myself in every mother or wife with whom I spoke, and what started out as a brief stint in recovery and rehabilitation to rack up the hours needed for graduation soon became the foundation for my life's work. I designed a specialized counseling service that family members or friends could come to; there they discussed and learned how to interact in a healthy way with their loved one: the alcoholic / addict.

My goal was to be of service to someone like me, who was once floundering around in the dark wondering what to do next, how to act, and what to say. I wanted to guide the family members or friends of the alcoholic / addict out of the hell they were in by teaching them how to use specific communication skills, to implement boundaries, and to restore their own respect and dignity while I helped them to understand what was going on in their loved one's life, whether in recovery or not.

After many years of working closely with people who have substance abuse issues and with their families, I wanted to share my personal and professional expertise through this book. I hope that it will become a useful tool in navigating the murky waters of addiction.

Congratulations on taking the first step in your own very important recovery.

I am not afraid of storms,
for I am learning how to sail my ship.
—LOUISA MAY ALCOTT

INTRODUCTION

If you are reading this book, then it is likely you are struggling with a loved one's addiction, addiction issues, or both. Addiction is an equal opportunity affliction, affecting the rich and the poor, the CEO and the blue-collar worker.

Here are some "sobering" facts about addiction in the United States from the National Council on Alcoholism and Drug Dependence Inc. (NCADD).

- 22.2 million people are addicted to alcohol and other drugs
- 15.4 million people are addicted to alcohol alone
- 3.6 million people are addicted to illicit drugs—no alcohol
- 3.3 million people are addicted to illicit drugs and alcohol
- 85,000 annual deaths are due to alcohol
- 18 percent of adults (1 in 5) have alcoholism in their family
- 38 percent of adults have 1 relative with alcoholism
- 76 million people (4 out of 10) are affected by alcoholism
- 10 million people are married to someone with alcoholism
- 27 million people are children of alcoholics, and an estimated 11 million are under the age of 18
- 13–25 percent of children of alcoholics develop alcoholism[1]

Addiction is considered the nation's number one health crisis. In addition, in one out of three failed marriages, the cause is attributed to addiction issues. Both statistical numbers are growing every day, month, and year. An emotional statistic reveals that for every one person addicted to alcohol or other drugs there are at least four family members or friends directly connected to their loved one's disease; that's quite a bit of pain and suffering.[2]

It seems there are endless pamphlets, websites, and other resources

coming from recovery programs, residential or outpatient clinics, rehabilitation centers, and sober-living housing to guide those with addiction
issues. Though many residential facilities offer family counseling, there is
little other than the Al-Anon Twelve-Step program to guide the families
of alcoholic/addicts through their maze of confusion in dealing with their
loved ones' addictions. As families, you are a special, silent group that deals
with frustration, anger, and heartache on an almost daily basis. You, too,
are desperate for help the same way that alcoholic/addicts feel their own
desperation.

Reclaim Your Life—You and the Alcoholic/Addict is a book specifically
written and tailor-made for you! Though there are many chapters written about the alcoholic/addict and how to better help you understand
their characteristics and dispositions, this book is *not* about them, how to
change them, or force them into recovery. It is about *your life* and the desire to gain back your self-esteem, self-respect, and dignity as you develop
new communication tools and boundaries.

This book was written out of a necessity to find answers that go beyond the obvious preaching about tough love, rescuing, or enabling. Specific communication techniques, role playing, theories, exercises, and actual case studies are discussed and described in detail throughout many of
the chapters. This book is designed to be an informative handbook as well
as a tutorial guide. Many concepts are repeated throughout, as applications
and key theories overlap. I would compare learning how to understand
and coexist with an alcoholic/addict to learning a new language.

My goal was to combine my personal history and my professional
expertise in the field of addiction so as to offer a book that is easy to read
and process—a reference for answers, suggestions, and comfort—not a
text that would be daunting and challenging to digest.

Please take your time when reading this. Counseling is not an exact
science; it is comprised of different points of view, experimentation, and
intuition. However, the concepts and theories that I explore have worked
for my clients; therefore, I wish to share them with you. This book took
years to write and was conceived in my heart. Know that I have lived every
line and every chapter, as I dealt with my own family and their world of
addiction. For years, every time the phone rang, I would catch my breath
and wonder … "Is that my loved one calling? Are they safe? Are they in
jail," or (all too often), "Are they dead?" When we love an alcoholic/ad-
dict, we all walk in the same shoes, with the same thoughts permeating our

brains. However, I was able to find some solace in knowing that "I didn't cause it, I can't control it, and I can't cure it," as it is repeated in many Al-Anon meetings.

It helps if you can remember that being a drug addict or alcoholic is not something that one aspires to become. Alcoholism was classified as a physical disease by the American Medical Association (AMA) in 1956. It is a disease that is never cured, only arrested.

I have heard many people say that their loved one is an alcoholic and, luckily, not a drug addict; therefore, their addiction is not as serious. Addiction is addiction, and can be described as "the same soup, just different bowls." However, having an issue with alcohol seems to be more socially acceptable since it is legal and many, many people drink—responsibly or not. With that said, practicing drug use seems to carry a stigma and is widely considered immoral, dirty, extremely dangerous, and of course, illegal. Generally speaking, I have found that not many alcoholics perform duplicitous acts like stealing from their families or friends in order to satisfy their addiction, whereas drug addicts have no qualms about kiting checks, pawning their family's jewelry, or even burglary.

Regardless, this book is not about bashing them or blaming them for your troubles and problems. Relationships require give and take from both parties, and sometimes give and take can be challenging for even the healthiest people. However, the added element of addiction can make these challenges even more difficult.

My hope is that this book will also be helpful and educational for anyone struggling with a substance addiction issue as well. They can, maybe for the first time, learn about their disease and its effects through the eyes of the family members or friends and maybe even appreciate the new road they are traveling to reclaim their own dignity and self-respect.

When reading this book, please keep four points in mind:

(1) I am not personally in recovery from alcohol or drug addiction. However, addiction is a family disease, affecting not only the alcoholic / addict, but the family and friends as well; hence, all participants are in recovery. Yet, it has been posed to me that if I am not in recovery, how can I know the behaviors and characteristics of a person addicted to alcohol or other drugs? I respect that query, but having personally lived with my own family's addiction issues and worked for years with a myriad of people in varying degrees of addiction and recovery, I have found that the similarities are so abundant, the data so uniform, that I don't need to be in their shoes

to share what I have learned. In addition, my observations are unfettered and unbiased. Someone who has been in recovery might have a different take or perspective, as recovery is personal, not objective.

(2) I respect that not all alcoholic/addicts fit the descriptions that I have predominately illustrated. It would be foolish of me to say that all people with a substance abuse issue, whether in recovery or not, are as I have portrayed. Everyone is different in their addiction and recovery process, and I apologize if I have offended anyone who has (successfully) traveled a different course.

(3) Throughout most of this book, I do not differentiate whether your loved one is in recovery or not. And I use the term alcoholic/addict whether your loved one has no desire to explore a clean and sober lifestyle or they have been committed to sobriety for twenty-five years. If concepts don't apply because they are working a healthy clean and sober program, then great; pick and choose what hits home and what doesn't.

(4) Though many of the concepts in this book can be implemented regardless of the age of the alcoholic/addict, this book is geared toward the family and friends who are dealing with loved ones of legal age and are capable of making decisions on their own. With that said, chapter 1, "The Most Common Routes Leading to Addiction," and chapter 17, "The Family Recovery Plan or Contract" are written for any age.

Seeing your loved one begin to entertain a substance abuse lifestyle or continue down such a path is scary and sad; there is no other way to put it. However, please keep an open mind, and try to adopt a good attitude. If you can do that, trust me, anything is possible in the land of recovery—yours and theirs.

Experience is not what happens to you,
it is what you do with what happens to you.
ALDOUS HUXLEY

Section One

IDENTIFYING AND UNDERSTANDING THE ALCOHOLIC/ADDICT IN YOUR LIFE

In order to understand (or try to understand) the disposition of the alcoholic / addict, this section is devised to breakdown some specifics about the nature of their disease, physically and emotionally. It starts with looking at some realistic options as to how an addiction may start. Characteristics and behaviors are then analyzed so that you can sift through what you may be experiencing with your interaction.

Please keep in mind that this section is not about condemning your loved one. On the contrary, the more knowledge you have, the better you may be able to comprehend, unemotionally, the many dispositions in their world of addiction.

Chapter 1

THE MOST COMMON ROUTES LEADING TO ADDICTION

The routes leading to dependency are one of the most confusing and misunderstood areas of addiction. Many parents pride themselves on having established a strong family unit and are baffled as to why their children have started dabbling with, or are regularly using, drugs or alcohol. Sometimes spouses, family members, and friends struggle to understand what prompted their loved one to walk down the road of addiction when they once viewed the person as content and grounded.

More often than not, people judge and admonish themselves, thinking that they somehow "did or did not do something" to propel a loved one toward self-destruction. Though difficult, it will be more beneficial if you can set aside your emotions and unnecessary flogging. I have known extremely involved and responsible parents whose children still found their way into addiction. Conversely, I've known parents who are unavailable to their children and substance abuse is not part of their youngster's life. Remember, that sometimes regardless of what we may or may not do as parents, we cannot control our children past a certain point. In addition, there can be families that have one child deep in addiction and the other living a healthy, normal lifestyle. Again, there can be no reasonable, concrete explanation, and we have to face the fact that it just might be a roll of the dice.

In this chapter, I am going to explore ten contributing factors that illustrate how and why someone may develop an addiction. Please realize that there are stimuli and unforeseen situations outside your control that can contribute to addiction. The more you understand about this disease, the more you might be able to scrape your face off the punching bag of blame. Here are contributing factors that lead to addiction:

- Family Involvement: The family is involved in drugs or alcohol.
- Neighborhood Involvement: The neighborhood is drug infested.
- Genetics: A latent "addiction gene" was inherited from a family member.
- Peer Pressure: The person uses alcohol/drugs as a way to belong, be accepted, or be popular.
- Emotional Pain: The person uses alcohol/drugs to escape from loneliness or depression.
- Low Self-esteem: The person uses alcohol/drugs to mask low self-worth.
- Boredom: The easily bored person uses alcohol/drugs for excitement and change.
- Trauma: The person uses alcohol/drugs to cope with a tragic physical or psychological event.
- Experimentation: The person's curiosity and interest in alcohol/drugs leads to addiction.
- Prescription Medication: A patient develops a reliance on a prescription drug.

Keep in mind that many of these dispositions toward addiction are interchangeable. Boredom and emotional pain are kissing cousins, just as the neighborhood and family involvement can be intertwined and trigger addiction.

Family Involvement:
The family is involved in drugs or alcohol.

It is very hard for a child to remain drug free if the family with whom they are living is abusing drugs or alcohol on a regular and open basis. An adult has the option of walking away; whereas, children are a captive audience. Instinctively, a child may know that this is not how a healthy family functions, but they grow so accustomed to the lifestyle around them that it is what they relate to best. We all know that children learn positive or negative habits by watching their parents as role models for behavior.

In addition, children can be easily influenced. If they witness an adult or someone they admire having a "good time" with alcohol or drugs, it may stand to reason that they, too, should expect the same good time if they indulge. It is hoped that children are taught responsible social drinking, and conversely, that they are taught what constitutes irresponsible and out-of-control behavior when it comes to alcohol intake. That said, there is nothing to be taught regarding how to be a responsible illegal drug user. Any degree of use can be dangerous, and I am of the opinion that responsible drug use is not realistic.

If this is the only exposure a child has had, then a parent's serious drinking problem or drug use issue often becomes footsteps for a child to follow. Keep in mind that family involvement in drugs or alcohol can take place among both low-income families and multi-millionaires, as drug and alcohol abuse know no socioeconomic boundaries.

Neighborhood Involvement:
The neighborhood is drug infested.

Unlike when the family itself is involved in drugs or alcohol, this pathway is the opposite scenario. A family often does everything in its power to protect its children from going down the road to addiction and self-destruction. Unfortunately, strong family structure and responsible, honest, or religious values are not guarantees against the constant barrage and temptations of a neighborhood with abundantly available drugs. For youngsters growing up in this environment, participating may be perceived as the only way to survive or be accepted.

Today, there is not a single neighborhood (whether affluent or underprivileged) where youths are impervious to the calling of drugs or alcohol. Parents must remember that they cannot cloak their children in suits of armor as they go to school or hang out with their friends. Hopefully, the history of open and honest communication parents have established with their children will prevail and keep them on the straight and narrow.

Genetics:
A latent "addiction gene" was inherited
from a family member.

A hot-button topic around substance abuse has been whether an "addiction gene" can be passed down from generation to generation. The question of nurture or nature seems to be constantly up for debate. According to the University of Utah:

> When scientists look for "addiction genes" what they are really looking for are biological differences that may make someone more or less vulnerable to addiction.
>
> It may be harder for people with certain genes to quit once they start. Or they may experience more severe withdrawal symptoms if they try to quit. Factors that make it harder to become addicted also may be genetic. For example, an individual may feel sick from a drug that makes other people feel good.
>
> But someone's genetic makeup will never doom them to inevitably become an addict; they just may need to be more careful.[3]

We inherit not just obvious physical traits, but deep-rooted emotional intricacies as well. Everyone has heard the phrases *he's a chip off the old block* and *the apple doesn't fall far from the tree*. If a person's talent in the arts can be passed down to the next generation, why can't addiction, depression, or even suicidal tendencies be passed down? Environment, upbringing, and a myriad of other entities shape us as individuals as we mature, but our inner core is closely linked to our genetic structure.

Whether you believe in the theory of "addiction genes" or not, the risk of developing addictive behavior is greater if the parents or grandparents have had addiction issues.

As a child matures to adulthood, the child (and their family) should always be alert to irresponsible or out-of-control actions that may indicate a predilection toward addictive behavior.

Peer Pressure:
The person uses alcohol/drugs as a way to belong, be accepted, or be popular.

Every person I've ever met—adult, teen, or child—wants to belong, to be accepted, and to be popular with their peers. The desire to belong and be accepted is a core human trait. Without it most people feel unsettled and uncomfortable, maybe even paranoid or fearful, regardless of age.

John Donne wrote, "No man is an island." This is true even if someone claims differently. Close relationships, familiarity, and camaraderie represent the very definitions of those warm and fuzzy feelings of belonging and being accepted.

Let's start with the child or teenager who spends the bulk of their waking hours at school. Though it may not be cool to admit it, most children have a desperate desire to be a part of a clique or group. If a child is able to find a satisfying and productive niche, then they will feel accepted and part of a special community. Not only is this experience good for a person's sense of well being, but it builds self-confidence and becomes a vital part of the formative years.

Participating in one's community instills a sense of commitment and accountability, not only to oneself, but also to others. As adulthood approaches, this environment helps set the stage for a self-assured career and establishes the skills necessary to function as part of a team.

Looking back on our own childhoods, we can probably remember the various groups that we and our peers belonged to. I may be stereotyping here, but there were always the brainy ones and the debate-team students; the nerdy, scientific set; and the lofty sports figures and oh-so-popular cheerleaders. So what happens when someone can't find the group that will provide a sense of belonging, acceptance, or popularity? Or what happens when someone has found a group they want to be a part of, but that group wants nothing to do with them?

As parents, our hearts break when we witness our children or teenagers starting to feel "less than," become self-critical, and possibly turn into their own worst enemies. Desperation might cause these children or teenagers to get sucked into doing something they know is wrong and possibly dangerous. Whether the behavior is to buy drugs, supply alcohol, or even to dabble in petty-to-serious criminal activity (shoplifting, robbery), confused and scared children and young adults may start to turn a deaf ear to instruction on morals, honesty, and values. In order fit in, be accepted, and supposedly be popular, they can begin to get caught up in a fast moving current of destruction. If these characteristics start to sprout and are not addressed, it is possible that the road to addiction may start here.

Emotional Pain:
The person uses alcohol/drugs to escape from loneliness or depression.

Let's now look at feeling lonely or depressed and wanting anything to take away the pain. After years of counseling in this field, I have found this to be one of the most common routes leading to addiction. Emotional pain is very real and part of everyday life. Whether you are a teenager, young adult, full-blown grownup, or in the geriatric set, living life on life's terms can be frequently painful. Turning to drugs and alcohol is an easy escape away from the pain and troubles of the day ... at least for the time being.

As previously mentioned, there are a number of routes that can become intertwined with each other. Wanting to belong, to be accepted, and to be popular could manifest as emotions of loneliness or depression if the desires are not fulfilled. Feeling lonely evokes an awareness of being cut off from others—mounting to feelings of bleakness and the inability to find any joy in life or its experiences.

The feelings of loneliness and depression are two very different sensations. Being lonely is more of a state of mind, and one's state of loneliness can change on a dime if one so desires to make the change. There can be a joy in solitude as opposed to the "down" of loneliness. There is also a difference between feeling lonely and being alone. When someone is alone, they are literally a party of one (solitude), and oftentimes that is the preferred choice. When someone is indeed feeling lonely—missing the company of others—someone has the ability, the choice, to move to a more populated venue. Often the cure is literally: get out and meet people. A lonely person can join a book club, take yoga classes, or join a volunteer group.

If someone counteracts loneliness by finding solace in drugs or alcohol, the outcome will always be destructive. Drugs and alcohol deliver a false sense of comfort, which in turn allows a temporary feeling of being no longer lonely. It is an illusory, unhealthy black hole that gets blacker and deeper with each foray.

As a treatment counselor, I assigned my clients to write a "Dear John" letter, or goodbye letter, to their drug of choice. In every letter, the addicts stated that their drug of choice had become their best friend, and when they were intoxicated or high, they were no longer feeling lonely. What could possibly be worse for genuine self-care and authentic long-term health than having your confidence buoyed or loneliness abated by such a deceitful and destructive companion?

Depression is different, and depending on the severity, depression affects people in different ways. We all have experienced to some degree a number of low times during our lives, and if someone is living life there are bound to be those low times.

Though these emotions are very real, the question is how do people successfully deal with them. Healthy, well-grounded individuals may lick their wounds for a while, draw upon the strength and love of their family and friends, seek professional help, or subscribe to safe, clinically proven medication to help offset this state of mind. Unhealthy responses to depression can make people think that drugs and alcohol are the only choices that will get them through their trying experiences.

Deep, ongoing depression or clinical depression is a very real disorder (versus being sad or experiencing minor bouts of depression). A clinical depression is categorized as having a depressed mood all day, diminished interest in pleasurable activities, significant weight loss, fatigue or loss of energy, and even recurrent thoughts of death or suicidal ideations. If not handled in a responsible, healthy way, these individuals are ripe for self-medication with drugs or alcohol, often stemming from an effort to take away the pain. Unfortunately, this path can leave someone as an addicted, semifunctioning, or even nonfunctioning individual. A vicious circle ensues, as depression leads to self-medication, and self-medication continues to fuel the depression.

Low Self-Esteem: The person uses addictive behaviors to mask low self-worth.

Low self-esteem describes a substandard evaluation or disappointing appraisal of one's self-worth. Development of self-esteem begins at the early stages of childhood and continues on through adulthood. It is a part of our lives forever, and depending on how we are feeling about ourselves, can put a positive or negative spin on our self-esteem. The family unit that is the focal point for the upbringing of a youngster can have the power either to instill a sense of strong self-worth or a self-image that is questionable or negative. Though more prevalent in early stages of development, anyone or anything can make an indelible impression.

I would like to believe that parents, siblings, guardians, friends, and teachers are circles of support for children, yet many people come from households that say, "You are so stupid." "Why can't you do anything right?," "You'll never amount to anything," or "Why aren't you more like your brother/sister ... look how well he/she is doing!"

Comments such as these are thoughtless, cruel, and produce so much negative energy that it takes substantially longer to "undo" the damage than the time it took to first chuck those slings and arrows. Such words forge indelible images in the mind of a child, and if not counteracted with loving, caring, and thoughtful communication, the words lead to a foundation of uncertainty, insecurity, and confusion. No matter what the age of the individual, these comments can live permanently in the subconscious and thwart any effort for that person to try and be successful at something they have been told they were too stupid to achieve or not capable of achieving. For example, if they were always told that they had two left feet and couldn't run successfully from their bedroom to the bathroom, they may feel that any athletic activity is a waste of time, or they may be ridiculed or laughed at. This feeling of low self-esteem can permeate other areas, like believing that their body or their looks are undesirable or that their brain power is insufficient. In both children and adults, low self-esteem can result in feeling stuck and having little or no motivation or energy. Everything becomes drudgery; hence, the potential for destructive behavior and the desire to escape into a world like addiction—where self-judgment is temporarily nonexistent—becomes a very powerful hook.

The mentality of someone with low self-esteem can sound like this: since there is no special ability needed to participate in alcohol consumption or illicit substance use, and no one cares if you like yourself or not, then why not go for it? What is left to lose? Here is an easy, effortless way to take a lack of self-esteem or self-worth and drink it away into blackouts or smoke it, snort it, or shoot it into oblivion.

Some people who are addicted to alcohol are shy, introverted people. Oftentimes, they suffer from low self-esteem issues, and they have relied on the effects of alcohol to help them come out of their shells and be more gregarious and approachable. The drinker may say, "Yeah, I need a few drinks in me to loosen me up." Be mindful that a person with alcoholic tendencies can easily go from a couple to ten or more drinks in one sitting.

Lack of confidence can be different than low self-esteem. For example, I have little or no confidence in my ability to be proficient on the computer, run a marathon, or paint a landscape; however, that kind of lack of confidence means that you might not be mentally up to a specific challenge, or you may not be physically able to do a particular task. A healthy person may say, "But so what? It's not my thing—who cares?"

The alcoholic / addict's lack of overall confidence can reinforce low self-esteem, and if someone *believes* they will fail, be ridiculed, or scorned no matter what the outcome, it becomes increasingly hard to try something new or accept any challenge.

Boredom:
The easily bored person uses drugs or alcohol for excitement and change.

As the saying goes: An idle brain is the devil's workshop. People with too much time on their hands may find themselves in hot, troubled waters. People who tend to be bored may also be weary or restless due to a lack of personal interest or motivation. They are bored with themselves, their jobs, and life.

Boredom usually stems from a state of complacency, void of challenges or creativity. Everyone gets bored now and then, but it is important to acknowledge the difference between changing that mood through healthy alternatives versus sitting around with friends passing the pipe for a few high-flying hits. This kind of reaction to boredom can ultimately lead to an antisocial, unhealthy path toward addiction.

Boredom takes some perseverance to shake off. It is a state of mind and requires committed determination to do something about it or change up the routine. People can form a habit of being bored, especially if no one expects anything from them, and in turn, they don't expect anything from themselves. Drugs and alcohol can seem like an acceptable choice to alleviate the routine of boredom. It only takes the easiest, quickest fix—requiring little or no effort to get high or drink—and poof … you're not bored anymore!

Trauma:
The person uses alcohol/drugs to cope with a tragic physical or psychological event.

Trauma is an incident or occurrence that happens inexplicably or without warning. It can happen to anyone of any age. It is categorized as an overwhelming life-changing experience. It is typically a physical or emotional shock that reverberates to the very fiber of one's being.

Trauma creates an imbalance in the emotional or mental system that is far beyond what is normal. Serious accidents, natural disasters, violent personal assaults, military combat, terrorist incidents, near-death experiences, or other major life alterations can all be considered traumatic, whether experienced or witnessed. A traumatic experience is personal, and one does not have to be privy to such a catastrophic event to feel that the world is suddenly collapsing around them. Being targeted for a crime like robbery, learning of the serious illness of a loved one, or discovering a sudden, unexpected revelation like learning of a mate's infidelity or desire for a divorce can unnerve the strongest of individuals. Also, keep in mind that people are different and one person may respond to trauma differently than the next person. Generally speaking, a person's response can result in intense fear, helplessness, or horror.

Though one may have an addiction issue before trauma strikes, the route to addiction may be easier to hook into as a result of the trauma. An addiction resulting from trauma is unlike the other gateways, as there is less of a conscious intent on deliberately getting high or intoxicated. That is, it's not a recreational choice based on peer pressure, nor meant to alleviate loneliness, boredom, or normal aspects of everyday life.

Everyone experiences varying degrees of trauma in their life. Similar to depression, trauma can lead to self-medicating (prescription or otherwise) to numb the pain or repress the memory of the event, which in turn can lead to dependency or addiction.

Post-traumatic stress disorder (PTSD) is a very real medical diagnosis categorized under anxiety disorders in the *Diagnostic and Statistical Manual of Mental Disorders (DSM)*. A person has acute PTSD if the duration of symptoms is less than three months, and PTSD becomes chronic if it persists over three months. Symptoms defined from the DSM-IV associated with PTSD are

- avoiding conversations associated with the trauma and not dealing with or confronting emotions and feelings
- avoiding certain people or places that may arouse memories of the incident
- feeling detached or estranged from society and friends, and considering interests, hobbies, or activities to be unimportant and not worth the effort to reincorporate into life
- difficulty in having, or continuing with, intimate relationships—this is especially true if a sexual or physical violation

upon the person is the reason for the trauma
- difficulty relaxing or sleeping soundly
- easily agitated or irritable—mercurial behavior or mood swings
- short-lived concentration or commitment to a task[4]

While a trauma is still fresh, it is important to engage a trained therapist who deals in that particular area before the experience can burrow and establish psychological roots. Do not give the trauma a chance to ferment or the injured party could take their recovery into their own hands with self-medication, which could lead to addiction. They may not be able or willing to stop the self-medicating once it starts. If this addictive behavior becomes established, the injured party now has two issues to deal with: the unfinished traumatic incident as well as the likelihood of substance addiction. Also, the trauma itself can be an excuse to continue the self-medication.

Trauma should never be taken lightly, especially if it involves a child. For youngsters, trauma can be anything from learning about their parents divorce to bathroom accidents or being picked on for something that might catch the amusement of fellow classmates. It doesn't have to be of great magnitude. To children, many events in their formative years become larger-than-life and therefore traumatic.

If parents know that a traumatic event has happened to a child, then they must take the appropriate action to ensure that the child is able to talk about the experience in a safe, comfortable environment. Don't downplay it or encourage the child to "just get over it and move on." Conversely, don't encourage the victim to make light of it or shrug it off, as they may be struggling internally. You don't know what could be rumbling around due to shame or embarrassment that might make it hard for a child to share the experience with you.

If trauma is not dealt with in its infancy, it can result in unfinished business. Trauma can rear its ugly head later in someone's life in the form of addiction or as an excuse for inappropriate or out-of-control behavior.

Experimentation:
The person's curiosity and interest in alcohol/drugs leads to addiction.

Most children, teenagers, and young adults go through some sort of experimentation phase on various levels. If your child is unfocused or feeling insecure or abandoned, they may have a stronger propensity toward acting out and experimenting with drugs or alcohol.

We have all heard our friends say, "Go ahead; don't be a chicken, try it!" Even if someone is already accepted within their clique or group of friends, they may jump at the chance to secure or improve their stature and confidence within a clique by accepting such a challenge. However, this experimental hook can sometimes present ethical, legal, or moral issues. The instincts of the child experimenting with alcohol or other drugs may kick in and reflect back to them that this is not exactly "kosher" or could produce questionable or even irresponsible behavior, yet they forge ahead anyway throwing caution to the wind.

Baiting and daring each other in adolescence goes with the territory—from the innocence of pressuring a friend to ask out a pretty classmate to betting on who can chug down the most beer in the fastest amount of time—challenging one another is par for the course. Drinking is usually the first tier of experimentation. It holds the allure of being perceived as cool and a false guarantee to having a good time. It's often a joke at adolescent parties to see who can become the most wasted. This experimentation can quickly become out of control and dangerous. It can elevate the "dorkiest" of students into a status of almost superhuman proportions because they can drink circles around the coolest or toughest of guys.

Experimentation can be construed as a rite of passage, but the questions to ask are concerned with how much to experiment, what to experiment with, and when does experimentation turn into addiction? Simply put, experimentation turns into addiction when one is no longer able to walk away but needs to fill that void on a regular basis in order to function.

I believe that drugs are a different matter than alcohol. Though a number of drug addicts talk about their drug of choice, they come to this conclusion because the other drugs they've tried don't satisfy their needs. They may not like the way cocaine makes them feel, or they may dislike the constant amped-up feeling of methamphetamine. The point is: people interested in drugs shop around until they find what satisfies them and meets their needs. When the "drug of choice" is found, they latch on; there's no need to acquire a taste for it or experiment further.

Prescription Medication:
A patient develops a reliance on a prescription drug.

One would be hard pressed to find an adult who has never taken prescription medication for physical or emotional pain. It's part of today's society to medicate what ails us. Prescription medication is designed to be easy and safe, but it can spark an addiction if not monitored. Most people in real physical or emotional pain who take prescription medication have honest and true intentions of alleviating their discomfort legally, with no intention or forethought of becoming addicted. I suffered from horrible back pain once, and when the doctors decided to administer some morphine, I certainly didn't think, "Oh boy, now I can become a drug addict legally with no repercussions."

Prescriptions are handed out today like flyers in Las Vegas. Whether you have a hangnail or an emotional disorder, it seems that there are too many practitioners ready with their pads to prescribe any kind of antidepressant, stimulant, or muscle relaxer. Not only can your body become addicted, but your psyche and emotional senses can be dependent on such drugs as well. Sometimes a psychological addiction is more profound (and more difficult to eradicate) than a physical one.

Being dependent on prescription medication has nearly become an acceptable addiction. Look at how many celebrities and athletes have admitted they are addicted to their painkillers for various injuries. Taking medication for sleepless nights or an old football injury are easy and plausible excuses. We tend to find ourselves saying, "Oh, well, that's okay and understandable. Poor people, look at their lives. They are under so much pressure or pain, so it's okay." Celebrities and sports figures can still remain popular and be role models since their prescription addictions are perceived as out of their control and not intentional. We should not be condoning this reasoning as an excuse for addiction.

I have listed the ten most common contributing factors toward addiction. You may have experienced something different with someone who has traveled a path toward an addiction to alcohol or other drugs. Regardless of how one gets there, addiction is addiction, and it should be treated as dangerous and possibly life threatening. Please don't take lightly any of these routes that may lead to addiction. If you see a loved one percolating toward destructive behavior, remember that not only is the prospective addict at risk but you and your family are as well. Sadly, very little cultivation is needed to take these scenarios from saplings to full-blown impervious trees that are extremely difficult to blow over or cut down.

When we long for life without difficulties,
remind us that oaks grow strong in contrary winds and
diamonds are made under pressure.
PETER MARSHALL

Chapter 2

THEORIES ABOUT ADDICTION AND RECOVERY

Many of my clients come to me and say that they don't know if their loved ones are addicted, and that even their loved ones say that they don't think of themselves as alcoholics or addicts. Everyone's definition is different. I hear, "My husband drinks too much, and he embarrasses me and himself when he's drunk. I think he's an alcoholic, but he swears he's not." I also hear, "My wife drinks too much wine when she's preparing dinner. I'm certain she has a drinking problem." But there are actual indicators that can take the guesswork out of determining if someone can define themselves as a person addicted to alcohol. Though the following questions are geared toward the prospective alcoholic, these questions can be adapted for the prospective drug addict as well.

Twelve Addiction Questions

Respectfully transcribed from, "The A.A. General Service Conference-Approved Literature," here are twelve questions that only the prospective alcoholic can answer. It might be interesting to see if you, as the family member or friend, would answer them the same way that the prospective alcoholic would.

1. Have you ever decided to stop drinking for a week or so but only lasted for a couple of days?

2. Do you wish people would mind their own business about your drinking—stop telling you what to do?
3. Have you ever switched from one kind of drink to another in the hope that this would keep you from getting drunk?
4. Have you had to have an eye-opener upon awakening during the past year? Do you need a drink to get started or to stop shaking?
5. Do you envy people who can drink without getting into trouble?
6. Have you had health problems connected with drinking during the past year?
7. Has your drinking caused trouble at home?
8. Do you ever try to get "extra" drinks at a party because you do not get enough?
9. Do you tell yourself you can stop drinking any time you want to, even though you keep getting drunk when you don't mean to?
10. Have you missed days of work or school because of drinking?
11. Do you have "blackouts"? (A "blackout" is when you have been drinking for hours or days and cannot remember anything that happened during that time.)
12. Have you ever felt that your life would be better if you did not drink?[5]

According to this questionnaire, if the prospective alcoholic answered "yes" to four or more of these questions, they are probably in trouble with alcohol. As previously stated, though these questions are specifically directed toward alcohol addiction, they can be asked regarding drug addiction as well.

Your History with the Alcoholic / Addict

Throughout my many years of counseling, I have assembled a number of theories that have a common behavioral thread regarding addiction—regardless of the drug of choice or someone's level of recovery. These have proved helpful to many family members as they continue their quest to better understand their loved ones and their addictions.

When a new client comes to see me, I present eleven questions to the family member or friend about the alcoholic / addict and their behavior. Like any responsible clinician, it's important for me to get as much information as possible regarding the history and interaction of all the participants.

Answer these questions as a worksheet for yourself, as they may shed some light on the successes and failures of recovery or lack thereof.

1. Have there been any recovery or rehabilitation attempts thus far? If so, how many times, and what were the outcomes?
2. Did the alcoholic/addict express a desire to take part in a rehabilitation program, or were they forced to attend through promises, threats, punishment, or legal sanctions?
3. What is the current state of mind of the alcoholic/addict regarding their addiction?
   a. Is this person in denial about the problem?
   b. Is this person on the fence about seeking help?
   c. Is this person ready to do whatever it takes to learn to live a clean and sober existence?
4. What is the psychological/emotional history of the alcoholic/addict?
   a. Is this person now, or has this person ever been diagnosed with bipolar disorder, post-traumatic stress disorder, or clinical depression?
   b. Is this person on medication? If so, for how long, and what have been the benefits and drawbacks?
5. Do other family members have an addiction issue?
   a. If so, are they in a treatment program?
   b. Do they live with, or have direct contact with, the alcoholic/addict?
   c. Does addiction run in the family—could they have inherited addiction genes?
6. Are you seeking professional guidance because of a final incident, a straw that broke the camel's back?
   b. What was the incident? Are there ramifications, either legal or personal, that have accompanied this final incident?
   c. Was there a new course of action set because of the incident?
   d. If so, how is that going?
7. How do you fit into the life of the alcoholic/addict?
   a. Are you still part of this person's life and in contact with this person?
   b. Have you removed yourself from this person's life?
8. Have you tried to impose your own recovery guidelines on the person? If so, what was the outcome?

    a. Was there any kind of agreement, contract, or understanding of rules and regulations between you and alcoholic / addict regarding their recovery?

    b. How successful or unsuccessful was this agreement? What worked? What didn't?

9. Are you seeking guidance to help in your own recovery, or are you hoping to find an answer or solution in order to "cure" your loved one?

10. Who (if anyone) in your intimate circle knows that you are seeking counseling? Are they supportive?

    a. Are other family members open to joining you in a team-counseling effort?

    b. Is the alcoholic / addict angry or resentful that you are seeking guidance? Or, if they found out, would they be angry or resentful?

    c. Would the alcoholic/addict be interested in participating with you in counseling?

11. Are you ready (really ready) to start a new life for yourself that would mean establishing stronger boundaries and more confident communication? Are you ready to challenge yourself with implementing new tools and actions toward the person in your life who is addicted to alcohol or other drugs?

These questions and answers should start you on the path of putting together a timeline for potential outcomes, successes, and failures. The most important questions are those listed for number 11, for regardless of your answers to the other ten questions, if you are not ready to change your course of direction with your loved one, then please wait until you are truly ready. Keep in mind that by now all the other options you have tried have not worked. So, wouldn't it make sense to try something new? Anyway, what have you got to lose?

I had a session with a woman who stated that she was fed up with her twenty-one-year-old son and his drinking. He had been to rehab already and was living at home with no job, no goals, and no responsibilities. He showed no interest in going to college or vocational training school, and his license had been suspended due to a DUI. He had been sponging off his mother and living this self-destructive pattern for a number of years. I asked her if she was ready to learn new communication skills and implement stronger boundaries. She questioned whether she could do it, and reported that she couldn't kick him out, as it would break her heart. That was our first and last session, as I couldn't help her if she wasn't ready.

Don't compromise what you hope to do or accomplish by being wishy-washy with your intentions, and even more importantly, with the ramifications. There will be more on that in later chapters.

I have a client who came to me exhausted and exasperated with the relationship she had with her twenty-six-year-old daughter. Using gentle prodding, I asked her if she was ready to establish strong boundaries and communications in dealing with her daughter, as for years her life had revolved around babysitting and cleaning up after her. If she was successful with extricating herself from the appendage of her child, what was she now going to do with her newfound freedom and independence? I pointed out that many family members become comfortable in their discomfort when it comes to their involvement with an alcoholic/addict. Since they have known nothing else for so many years, they become used to having their loved one's addiction issues as the center of their lives as well. Though deploring being the enabler, codependent, and rescuer (chapter 10) this is a role they have become used to, and it might be difficult to give up or change.

This new approach to life might take some getting used to. The new time and energy that comes from not having to fix or take care of the alcoholic/addict is actually quite daunting for many people, but at the end of the day it's very much worth the effort!

Four Dispositions of Alcoholic Consumption

If you live with an alcoholic, then chances are that you are already too familiar with the personality changes your loved one goes through when drinking. Nonetheless, I have put together four dispositions or stages that the alcoholic is likely to experience before the night (or day) is over.

1. **The first stage** often finds the drinker happy, fun, easy-going, and cheerful. They may be perceived as the life of the party. For a shy or quiet person, alcohol can be the key to loosening up. For the tense or stressed personality, alcohol is the key to unwinding. Whatever the excuse or reason (and there is always one), the drinker has become accustomed to their own personal happy hour.

2. **The second stage** finds the drinker sitting on the pity pot. They will bemoan the fact that no one understands, respects, or appreciates all that they are doing. The drinker will accept some responsibility for drinking too much, but then they will find justification for their actions by blaming you, the job, or circumstances of life, whether big or small (from not getting what they wanted for dinner to being fired).

3. **The third stage** finds the drinker becoming belligerent, angry, argumentative, and sometimes even paranoid. The drinker can turn violent if they believe that their needs are not being met, or that they are being undermined or talked about. At this stage, the slightest provocation can turn into an explosion of a grand magnitude.

4. **The fourth stage** finds the drinker blacked out or passed out. For the moment, the drama is over, and the drinker will sleep it off—that is until the next day or the next time they drink. The drinker awakes embarrassed, apologetic, probably feeling sick, and *swearing* that they will never drink again. Though the intentions are most likely genuine, if they are not really ready to embrace a program of sobriety—doing whatever it takes to learn to live a clean and sober lifestyle—then when physically feeling better, the drinker will return to an alcoholic disposition. The drinker may start out slowly, working diligently to curb the drinks to a respectful handful, but eventually they are back up to full throttle.

I once had a friend that fit stages one through three perfectly. Since I didn't live with her, I didn't know when stage four kicked in, but I was sure it did at some point. Like clockwork, she would call on an almost daily basis and leave a message for me to call her back. I thought she had a drinking issue, so I would always look at my watch before responding to the call. Depending on the time, I could be fairly accurate at knowing what stage she might be in with her alcohol consumption. If I called in the afternoon between four o'clock and five o'clock she would be in the "happy" stage. If it was after that time, then I learned to wait until the next morning. No matter what she had to tell me, if it was after five o'clock I was certain to get an earful of whatever was bothering her that day, and the conversation would morph into a one-sided, angry narrative having nothing to do with me or the reason for her call in the first place.

I tell you this because it is important for you to learn to identify these stages of inebriation. Being aware of these stages will help you to prepare and be proactive.

The Pyramid of Change

Many of my clients can be very hard on themselves, flogging with self deprecation for their "stupidity" in ignoring the warning signs or failing to do something about unacceptable behavior before it was too late. I know for me with my own loved one's addiction, I would see it, but didn't want to acknowledge it. I found that *I* came up with as many excuses for their behavior as *they* came up with excuses for their behavior. And sometimes it's not so obvious or can be well hidden.

I have formulated what I call **The Pyramid of Change.** These are six tiers of disposition for the alcoholic / addict that can slowly creep up on the most unsuspecting family member or friend. If you are aware of the tiers, you may know what to expect and allow yourself a different outcome.

Tier #1. Whether you are in a new relationship or one that has clocked in a number of years, you have started to become aware of your loved one's unfamiliar behavioral patterns, and something tells you that things are just not right. You are beginning to witness little, almost insignificant, spikes of illogical behavior that you accept as mood swings, a phase, or simple frustrations regarding work, school, or just daily occurrences. It is no big deal—a passing interruption in what you are used to as a normal, stable life. You have a watchful eye out, but chances are you may ignore it and continue on with your life as usual.

Tier #2. You are aware that what felt unsettling in Tier #1 is becoming more of a reality and hard to just slough off as a bad day at the office or losing a football game. Broken promises and questionable or irresponsible behavior start creeping up more and more. Though you are suspect about the excuses, you accept them, and your loved one convinces you that as soon as "A, B, or C" is taken care of then their rocky ship will stabilize.

Tier #3. The situation has become more untenable or out of control, and the person's actions are now interfering with your day-to-day responsibilities and routines. Financial and/or legal ramifications may now be part of the landscape. The prospective alcoholic/addict concedes that their behavior has caused more problems and again guarantees to right the wrong. The person is genuinely sorry for their actions and promises to take the necessary steps to fix the problem. You trust them, as you feel you have no choice, but you are uneasy and uncertain about what tomorrow might bring. You see some change, and the skittish behavior is tethered. You may start to breathe a sigh of relief, but nonetheless you are anxious.

Tier #4. It seems that over time the commitment made in Tier #3 is losing momentum and the addictive disposition is starting to creep back. Bad choices equal bad outcomes. Out-of-control behavior and irresponsible actions are beginning to accumulate into substantial wreckage. It's all starting to pile up higher and higher. Your patience is worn thin, and you can see the physical and emotional toll your loved one's addiction has caused you, and possibly other family members as well. The alcoholic/addict professes their need for professional treatment and cannot get clean and sober without that help. With heartfelt conviction, the person convinces you that this time it will be different because they don't want to lose you or the family.

Tier #5. Regardless of what kind of rehabilitation program your loved one is in, or how strongly they are committed to it, somewhere along the way the sobriety of the alcoholic/addict will be tested. Often the person truly believes they have a strong handle on a clean and sober lifestyle, yet they may start to take it for granted and become complacent. Instead of committing to the hard, cold fact of never again forming an alliance with their drug of choice, the alcoholic/addict tries to convince themselves (and you) that by practicing moderation the alcohol or illicit substance can be welcomed back. The alcoholic/addict appreciates and praises what they have learned in recovery and now professes to know their limit before things get out of hand. Alternatively, this person may switch teams: since alcohol was not the problem, they can become a social drinker, or swear off "hard drugs" and just use marijuana. You are anxious about this statement, because by now you know that this theory is impossible, and only total abstinence from all drugs and alcohol will work. In all probability, you have been given this speech before.

Tier #6. The alcoholic/addict has unfortunately returned to their full-blown addiction. Hopefully, you have had enough of bumping along the bottom with broken promises and unfulfilled commitments. As heart-breaking as this is, it is time to present your loved one with walking papers; they need to decide whether to live a clean and sober life on their own terms, their own way without your involvement, or a drug/alcohol-infested life. You proclaim *enough is enough!* and feel confident that you have done all that you could with support, patience, and love. Whether it is your child, spouse, sibling, relative, or friend, you are out of gas. You have been down every road imaginable to help your loved one with this addiction, but you are now a shell of yourself and barely have the energy to put one foot in front of the other anymore. You state, through a veil of tears, that you love the person deeply, but they can no longer be part of your life until they have taken control of their addiction. You both know that all credibility has been lost, and it is time to start over at square one if there is to be any possibility of re-establishing a relationship in the future.

The C.A.R.D. Acronym

So, now that you have drawn a line in the sand for the alcoholic/addict to adhere to, what does it look like to re-establish honest behavior and start rebuilding trust? What does it look like not only to you and the family, but to anyone who has direct contact? I have put together an acronym I call **C.A.R.D.** (Credibility. Accountability. Responsibility. Dependability.) This concept is discussed again in chapter 12, "Allow the Alcoholic/Addict to Rebuild Their Life." I have used this as a benchmark for the alcoholic/addict who is in recovery and looking to build better communications and relationships with their family members and friends. In turn, family members and friends should expect these changes as well.

Keep in mind that while enmeshed in addiction, your loved one might have lied, cheated, or performed other duplicitous acts. The alcoholic/addict is a very selfish person—as is the disease—and unfortunately, addiction brings out the worst in everyone.

An enormous part of the recovery process and progress is built around the alcoholic/addict starting to pull themselves up by their own bootstraps. Making honest decisions, weighing options, thinking clearly through possibilities, are all ways to start to rebuild a new life by first repaving the road of trust.

The more your loved one can come up with a self-conceived game plan, even if it turns out to be a poor one, the more they will learn and gain through building a *personal recovery* as well as a *clean and sober recovery.* Alcoholic / addicts need to reconnect with themselves and start to trust their own core instincts for planning and developing a road map toward achieving all their goals. Even if you don't agree with the path they have set out for themselves, or if that path ultimately turns out to be the wrong one, let your loved one march to their own drummer.

The C.A.R.D. acronym refers to key actions that should be implemented by those in recovery when re-establishing important personal traits for themselves, and in turn, demonstrating to their family members and friends their commitment to rebuilding the relationship.

C.A.R.D.
Credibility = trustworthy
Accountability = answerable for
Responsibility = fulfilled obligation
Dependability = reliable

These character traits are obviously interchangeable and jointly represent that the alcoholic / addict is starting to become grounded and focused in recovery as well as life. These are actions of determination and are impossible to carry out on a regular or continual basis if a person is still wrapped up in their addiction.

In working with the alcoholic / addict, I've never encountered a client who has said "yes" when asked if they deserved to be trusted while in active addiction or in the first few months of recovery. The alcoholic / addict realizes that restoring trust takes time. A person in recovery generally understands that when working on a solid, grounded recovery program, as well as embracing life, trust will slowly, but surely, start to be restored among family members, friends, employers, and partners.

In a sober state, the alcoholic / addict will reflect upon what their irresponsible and out-of-control behavior was like and what that behavior put others through because of the addiction. In an odd way, alcoholic / addicts in recovery look forward to rebuilding that trust, for they want to prove to their support team as well as to themselves that they are capable of being trusted again. Most recovering alcoholic / addicts genuinely want to be good parents, sons, daughters, friends, or spouses to the ones they love and are desirous of mending the past. It's important for family and friends to give this process a substantial amount of time—at least six months of responsible, accountable, behavior is needed before trust is gently and cautiously embraced again.

In my practice, I have often heard a client say that their son or daughter, husband or wife, had been doing well, but that this or that happened, which wasn't their loved one's fault. The person in recovery was unable to fulfill a promise or commitment that was made because of someone else or due to circumstances out of their control.

If there is a legitimate reason (an emergency or other out of the ordinary occurrence) where the bond of trust might be somewhat compromised, then fine; but if not, start your own clock of trust over again, and your loved one should do the same. There is nothing wrong with family or friends asking themselves periodically if their loved one is still fulfilling the C.A.R.D. program.

In time, it is hoped that they will find their stride, reconnect with society, and prove to everyone (but most importantly to themselves) that they are restoring credible, accountable, responsible, and dependable behavior through a clean and sober lifestyle. The person in recovery will revel in re-establishing that their word is their bond.

These are just a handful of common theories I have put together to help you ascertain the disposition of the alcoholic / addict. You may relate to all of them or just a few, but there is usually a common thread running with addictive behavior and the concerns and needs of the family members and friends.

You never find yourself until you face the truth.
PEARL BAILEY

Chapter 3

CHARACTERISTICS OF THE ALCOHOLIC/ADDICT

If you are already more than familiar with the behaviors and characteristics of an alcoholic/addict, then why do I point them out? After all, you have probably lived with them for years. I have found that there can be comfort in hearing or reading that what you thought might be unique to you turns out to be a universal situation. The validation of knowing that others are experiencing the same scenarios that you are can bring on a resolved nod of the head or a deep comforting sigh—a recognition that you are not alone.

We are all aware of the behavioral differences between someone in a sober state and someone who is high or intoxicated. As previously stated, you may choose not to see your loved one's addiction and dismiss it as a teenage rite of passage or a bad couple of days (or weeks) at the office. However, your concern grows when your child goes from an "A" student to one who is barely passing, or when you see sudden irresponsible behavior in a friend, mate, spouse, or sibling. Confusion abounds and you soon begin to seek answers as to what lies behind your loved one's thinking and this new behavior. The uncomfortable word *addiction* now rents more space in your brain than ever before.

In order to help you understand what makes the alcoholic/addict tick, this chapter discusses some typical behaviors and characteristics. This information is not intended as a way to demonstrate to that person how informed you are, but rather to empower you with your own knowledge and to ultimately give you a more confirmed state of mind.

After years of personally loving, living, and working with alcoholic/addicts in my own life and private practice, I have continually observed behaviors exhibited whether in recovery or not. The behaviors that are more specific to active addiction will be obvious, as will the ones that surface once someone is in recovery. I have listed these in no particular order, and have penned them Typical Addictive Behavior (TAB). They may all pertain to your loved one, or only one or two of these may apply.

1. The comfort zone:

Those who are active alcoholics or drug addicts can be uncomfortable around strong, confident, or grounded individuals. They don't want to be in the company of secure or stable individuals, since using illicit drugs is usually not of interest to them and they are probably able to control their drinking. A nonaddicted person is only waving a red flag at the alcoholic/addict, showing how out of control their behavior really is. That is the last thing the alcoholic/addict wants to know. So, controlling their environment is important to them. Rarely do alcoholics enjoy drinking substantial amounts of alcohol around someone who is not drinking at all or around someone who doesn't partake in the same consumption of liquor. Most who are addicted to alcohol drink with other alcoholics or drink in solitude. They may start out as social drinkers, but over time, alcoholics often prefer to drink alone in the safe haven they have developed for themselves. This way, no one will monitor their intake or judge them. Their alcohol can eventually become their best friend; therefore, they don't need any human counterpart to provide company or make them feel complete.

Drug addicts are interested in how their drug of choice can make them feel. Their highs will not be enhanced or diminished whether they indulge as a party of one or twenty-one. Drug addicts may not be as social as alcoholics, and they stay in the comfort zone with their drug of choice.

2. Picking and choosing their recovery path:

In working with many people who are addicted to alcohol or other drugs and are striving toward recovery, I have found that when they are 100 percent ready to turn their life around, they will eagerly seek help in doing that. Whether their path consists of residential, outpatient, or a Twelve Step addiction recovery program, they realize their own life is out of control and they need help and guidance from someone or something else.

Yet, all too often, the alcoholic/addict who has not yet come to the conclusion that their life is unmanageable may not be ready to give in. The alcoholic/addict may have one foot in the door of recovery and one foot still out. I have told my clients that when they hear their loved one say, "I will do whatever it takes to learn to live a clean and sober existence," *period*, and not, "I will do whatever it takes to learn to live a clean and sober existence *my way* then they can be confident that the door to a new beginning is probably not yet a reality.

People with drug and alcohol addictions who want to pick and chose their recovery plan are still holding on to their ego and pride, and a true and honest recovery will be iffy at best. These are alcoholic/addicts who will work on what they want, when they want. If they feel that they don't have to do something specific, or that it's not for them, then that is that. For example, your loved one might decide that a few weeks at a residential treatment center is all they need, even though the program is designed for sixty or ninety days. This obviously is irresponsible thinking, and they are deciding what they want versus learning the best and healthiest path toward living a clean and sober lifestyle.

I know many people who have embraced the Twelve Steps of Alcoholics Anonymous (A.A.), have clocked in substantial years in sobriety, and still continue to attend meetings in order to keep themselves honest and accountable. However, the alcoholic/addict who picks and chooses a personal recovery plan will find it convenient to say, "Twelve Step meetings are not for me. I'm not as bad off as those people. I can't relate to anyone there," or "I'm not going to share my personal story out loud—it's nobody's business, and I can do this myself." It becomes a bit like a Chinese menu: one from column A (I will do this) and two from column B (I won't do that).

One has to make time and agree to a bona fide emotional and psychological commitment to recovery. Just deciding to stop drinking or using drugs is not what recovery is about. Freeing the body of the physical addiction is only the tip of the iceberg, but the emotional and psychological one is still in full bloom. I will discuss this concept in more detail in "The 'dry drunk'."

3. Sabotage:

Sometimes, when alcoholics start to get a handle on their recovery, or the going gets too good, they sabotage it. Though they freely admit that they are healthier and feel better, this new way of life can feel unfamiliar and uncomfortable. They might have difficulty trusting that it is good and will continue to remain so as long as they stay on a clean and sober path. Too often, with the slightest hiccup they retreat to what's familiar, even when they know it's detrimental or may produce substantial wreckage.

Alcoholic / addicts may not feel they deserve some of the good things that are happening to them, and this can be at the root of their self-sabotage. In addition, the expectations of others that they will "keep up the good work" can be a lot of pressure.

My client Cathy was working hard on trying to make her marriage work with her recovering alcoholic husband. He felt that he was moving mountains to make himself better and asked what her part was in doing the same. She was not in a recovery program, so she was confused as to what "her part" even was. Her husband would grill her on what she was doing to be a better wife and friend in order to make their marriage more solid. In essence, he claimed that she was falling short on doing "her part." In order to do her part and make her husband happy, Cathy sought out counseling, attended more Al-Anon Twelve Step recovery meetings, vigilantly watched her tone and attitude, and avoided areas of communication that might be explosive for them. Yet, no matter what Cathy did, her husband wasn't satisfied with her efforts. We came to the conclusion that her husband was so bent on sabotaging the relationship that she couldn't satisfy him, no matter what she did or said. Her husband was constantly raising the bar by making it impossible for her to reach any goal that would be acceptable. Ultimately, they went their separate ways; he successfully sabotaged his relationship with a loving, caring partner and friend. He had difficulty trusting that things were good and healthy in his life. She believed she had been supportive and attentive to her husbands needs, but just could not please him or help him find his level of contentment. She even asked him once why he continued to bite the hand that loved him.

I experienced an incidence of self-sabotage when my own loved one was going through recovery. When my daughter was in a special high school out of state for her addiction issues, cutting, and eating disorders. I was pleased to learn that she was making good progress. An important party was planned in California, and I really wanted her to attend, as did she. The school granted permission, and I believed we were both looking forward to the event. However, a few days before she was supposed to leave, she started acting out at school and was no longer permitted to come. I was disappointed. When I asked her what had happened and why she couldn't come, she was very vague with her answer and grunted an apology. Later, I learned that she probably sabotaged the situation (either consciously or unconsciously). Maybe she was nervous about being outside her comfort zone of school; or she felt she would have to "perform" before a room full of strangers; or maybe the trepidation of being questioned ("How are you? When are leaving there? Are you clean and sober?") might have been too much for her to process with confidence and security.

For the "normie" or healthy one, it is hard to imagine someone working hard to sabotage something good and comforting, yet it happens. Sometimes, no amount of professional counseling, Twelve Step recovery programs, or good old-fashioned talking between each other will do the trick. I believe the alcoholic / addict understands that they are sabotaging a situation, but sadly, just can't help themselves—until often it is too late to change direction.

Sometimes when alcoholic / addicts plan on self-sabotaging they justify it with, "It's all your fault. You won't do what I need you to. I'll show you. You'll be sorry." Deep down inside they realize that kind of thinking is ridiculous, and that they alone are responsible for their own actions. However, pointing the finger at someone else as the catalyst for this reckless behavior makes it palatable and gives them fuel to follow through with their intentions.

4. Extremes:

Many alcoholic / addicts have led a life of extreme highs and lows, and this has prevented them from achieving comfort in the normalcy of daily life. A middle ground of feeling okay and having a general, commonplace sense of purpose and accomplishment may not be good enough. When others might feel content, an alcoholic / addict may experience feeling unsettled or uneasy with what's next.

Maybe in young adulthood these individuals never learned how to roll with the punches, taking the good days with the bad; therefore, they found themselves experiencing mood swings or thoughts that lent themselves to extreme highs or basement lows—and subsequently they escaped to their addiction.

Similar to highs and lows, sometimes the alcoholic / addict can look at things as just black or white, leaving out the entire landscape of gray. There is so much area in between to ponder, process, and facilitate, but the alcoholic / addict may not yet have the life skills or confidence to do that. Remember that for some time the person with addiction issues has retreated to a world of escapism—a world with only an attitude of flight and not fight. Recovery takes patience and a willingness to break that old cycle. Hitting the pause button and stepping back to look at some other options to solve problems (finding the gray area) would be a productive way for the alcoholic / addict to stop thinking that the only answers are either black or white.

The alcoholic / addict who has a propensity toward anger needs to calm down enough to focus on that middle ground. Being able to step back and to calmly and rationally assess the situation and weigh the options and outcomes is imperative to a healthy recovery program. However, they may first need to get a handle on that anger before learning to live comfortably and responsibly in the gray area.

5. Getting needs met:

In this new substance-abuse-free life, the alcoholic / addict may feel they are not getting their needs met. Additional frustration might come from not knowing what their new needs are, or how to ask to have these needs met. They may lack the communication tools and skills needed to deal with and understand these new changes and how they relate to themselves as well as their family and friends.

Alcoholic / addicts were most likely the center of attention for many years, as they and their disease took center stage. A worried mate or spouse, worried parents and family members, and worried friends probably have spent countless hours wondering where their loved ones were or what they were doing. Many more hours were spent begging and pleading for them to change their lifestyle. Still more hours were invested in varying methods of cajoling, negotiating, or even punishing in an effort for them to seek recovery in counseling or rehabilitation programs.

Throughout this time, the alcoholic / addict was receiving attention—often negative attention, but negative attention is better than no attention at all. Now with this newfound sobriety, your loved one may feel that they are not getting the same amount of attention they've been used to. In reality, the needs are probably being met, but in a different, healthier way. They may not be used to it or may be uncomfortable and become unbalanced with the difference between getting needs met in sobriety versus being the center of attention while in addiction. Though they may have no idea about how to go about getting their new needs met, the memory of an old need for negative attention still burns and therefore presents a conflicting and confusing mental state. With the alcoholic / addict practicing a clean and sober lifestyle, now family, friends, and co-workers might be picking up the pieces of their lives and starting to go about their own business. Before, the alcoholic / addict was the nucleus for all involved with their lifestyle. Acting-out behavior may be their way of bringing the focus back to them instead of working toward a fair share of attention in a healthy, productive way.

6. The bully:

When people do not feel good about themselves, they can be masterful at rearranging an argument to deflect it away from themselves and on to another. The alcoholic / addict can do this better than anyone, and the family members and friends can find themselves the dumping ground for their diatribe. The intention is to bring you down to their level of unhappiness, discomfort, or indecision. After all, misery loves company.

Dialogue can easily begin to sound like this: "Your tone, attitude, and lack of understanding is the reason why I do what I do. You need to change or you could be the reason why I continue to drink, use drugs, or relapse."

At that moment, the alcoholic / addict is unhappy with themselves, and when uncomfortable in their own skin, it is easier for them to blame someone else, anyone else, than to stop and examine their own problems. Sometimes this mental anguish that they inflict on their family members or friends can be just as painful as physical abuse. Surely not premeditated, it can nevertheless be easy for them to spout out mean, condescending barbs such as, "No one likes you," "You don't care about anyone but yourself," or "You're stupid and have no idea what you're talking about."

All of this is a way for them to deflect what they may be thinking or feeling about themselves and camouflage it by turning it back on innocent, unsuspecting family members or friends. Anyone would call this "bullying behavior," but the alcoholic / addict displays this disposition substantially more frequently than the "normie" or healthy individual. It's easy for them to revert to becoming a "bully" when they are uncomfortable with a scenario, questioned about their actions, cornered with no verbal or physical escape route present, or feeling that they may not be getting their way.

The "dry drunk" is often described as a bully. The combination of not being able to drink responsibly and not dealing with painful emotions that were masked for many years through alcohol (or drugs) can result in that person presenting and communicating with a brittle, caustic demeanor, tone, and attitude.

As I discuss in chapters 5 and 6, the best defense one has is to not engage and walk away. It is a common saying in the recovery community that when the alcoholic / addict is pointing a finger at you, there are three pointing back at them.

When the dust finally settles, they generally feel terrible about their abusive behavior. They recognize and know they've been "bad" and are often ashamed and embarrassed. As a result, their attitudes are subdued and remorseful. It becomes very easy for a family member or friend to feel vulnerable and forgive out-of-control behavior, possibly for the umpteenth time. You want to believe they mean well and have learned a valuable lesson; hey, what loving soul would not want to forgive someone who comes with hat in hand? In addition, we have all heard that admitting one's failures is half the battle.

Please take caution that the contrite, personal flogging of your loved one's admission of being wrong, having failed, and knowing they can do better does not result in you once again saying, "That's okay; I appreciate you admitting that you were wrong." The alcoholic / addict may have gotten used to playing this card like a professional poker player. Unless you see real and genuine improvement, this disposition may be short lived. The bully can once again rear its ugly head, as this is a comfortable place to retreat to and plant fresh land mines all over again to the unsuspecting family member or friend. Bullying behavior is never acceptable. If this person's respect for you is not maintained, make sure you have strong and confident boundaries and consequences in place that they are fully aware of.

7. **Maturity level:**

People who have been in addiction for the majority of their lives re-enter the world of sobriety with some distinct disadvantages. One is that their level of maturity and basic life lessons have been shut down from almost the moment their addictions took hold. For alcoholic / addicts who started seriously drinking or using in their twenties and are now in recovery in their forties, chances are that they will pick up life where they left off. Hence, the forty year old, due to all those years of drinking or using, will likely have a case of arrested development. They might have avoided the normal maturation that comes from things like job responsibilities, career moves, intimate relationships, and raising a family.

As the recovery process gets underway, the alcoholic / addict realizes that their personal growth has been compromised, and they may struggle with finding the patience and ability to wade through the adaptation of this new lifestyle. They have been in a sort of time capsule and now emerge years later. Recovery may become compromised if frustration in dealing with life on life's terms causes this person to ultimately sabotage all the healthy development they have worked so hard to accomplish.

Hopefully, once they feel that they are grounded in their recovery programs, they will want to start making up for the time that was lost due to addiction during their teenage, young adult, or adult years. Obtaining a counselor or therapist for personal issues that are not related to addiction might be the first step in forging through emotions and past challenges.

They may even entertain getting a mental health exam and open up to the possibility of prescribed medication that might make that journey easier. Alcoholic/addicts are still clean and sober even if they are getting acupuncture treatments or taking medication for attention deficit disorder, post-traumatic stress disorder, or symptoms of depression. These are all tools that can help people who are addicted to alcohol or other drugs (or anyone) work toward stabilizing their lives.

8. The "dry drunk":

Clients have often come to me thrilled that their loved one has stopped drinking, yet they report that their partnership is as brittle as tinder and inexplicably worse than before. Confusion abounds as you both desire sobriety, and yet now that it is here, you wonder why the relationship seems to be on rockier ground than when the alcoholic was drinking. This is the world of the dry drunk, whether an alcoholic or drug addict.

So, what is a "dry drunk"? Other than the obvious (one that is not actively consuming alcohol), a dry drunk is a person addicted to alcohol or other drugs who may have embraced a recovery program to abstain from alcohol (or drugs), but has not yet worked on the other elements to round out a comfortable and complete clean and sober lifestyle.

If any of us were to stop participating in something that we were used to doing for years, something that was a substantial part of our daily existence, we would need additional help emotionally and psychologically in working through the absence of such an important element. This is especially true if that element is physically addictive. We must remember that alcohol or drugs were the fiber of an addict's existence for some time and a substantial if not total embodiment of their being.

Alcoholic / addicts need to be responsible for all aspects of their recovery. This can only happen through a Twelve Step recovery program, residential rehabilitation center, outpatient facility, sober living housing, or a professional addiction counselor, otherwise their growth in recovery could be stunted with only one piece of the pie in check—being physically clean and sober.

These people can be termed "dry drunks" if they only work on the clean and sober aspect of their recovery. If the emotional/ psychological side is void of attention, then they may find themselves complacent, irritable, easily annoyed, or quick to anger—they will defend and justify themselves at the slightest questioning. The dry drunk may not be open or willing to do the additional heavy lifting it takes to examine the emotional and psychological inner core in the effort toward a complete and honest recovery. Because of that they may use you as a punching bag for their frustration and discontent.

Here are seven characteristics of the dry drunk that you may be very familiar with:

- Resentment aimed at the spouse, parent, or whoever has apparently made them "stop drinking or else ..."
- Frustration that because of their drinking they may not have realized goals, dreams, or passions—even the simple pleasures of what life has to offer may have eluded them.
- Anxiety that it's too late—and doubt about whether they are even capable of achieving their goals or dreams
- Regret that because of their drinking, they were unable to sustain a loving relationship with a partner, and subsequently they have no family of their own
- Remorse about the years that were wasted because of drinking
- Fear of venturing out or challenging themselves because their expectation of failure is so dominant in their mind that they may not have had any normal life experience with failure and success, which in turn would have made them stronger, wiser, and more confident to tackle new and

creative tasks.

- Envy of others for their stick-to-itiveness, perseverance, and strength; smoldering resentment of those close to the alcoholic / addict who are diligently staying focused and committed to their task at hand

If the alcoholic / addict is not dealing with these dispositions, then you may feel like you need to walk on eggshells, watching your every move and word, as you don't want to incite an angry exchange. I have heard clients say that at least when their loved one was drinking they knew what to expect. You can start to feel damned if you do, damned if you don't. Irresponsibility, anger, and resentment now seem to go with the person who was an active alcoholic as well as the dry drunk. Personally, I've been there with my own loved one, and it's not a comfortable place to be.

I work closely with clients with addiction issues to dig into their past to try and unlock some of the emotional and psychological baggage that continues to hamper them from moving from a dry drunk to a healthy, functioning friend, mate, parent, or co-worker. An open mind and a good attitude are imperative for those who have addiction issues to deal with their painful past and what might have brought them to that road to addiction. I believe that one who is committed to a full landscape of recovery will be desirous of tackling the unfinished business that could hamper their success if not dealt with.

I think one of the keys for personal and emotional success is to find something to be passionate about. While dealing with the emotional and psychological turmoil that triggered and sustained the addiction in the first place, the alcoholic / addict needs something to replace the total encompassing attention they gave to their drug of choice. In turn, this new interest might quell a lazy disposition, knee-jerk anger, resentments toward another, or even relapse.

My client Davis shared with me that he built a fire pit in his backyard. We discussed how he might expand this accomplishment into a passion of vision and beauty for others. Sketching other fire pits, exploring quarries to seek out different materials, and designing a website and marketing flyers blew some exciting and confident wind in his sails. He could then turn his energy and attention away from functioning as a dry drunk and toward something that allowed him to feel good about each little accomplishment that went into building his new venture.

My client Robert had a dream of opening a breakfast-only restaurant. Working weekends as a short-order cook continued to fuel his passion. His focus became more energized as he increased his knowledge of the food business and started putting together business plans and creative marketing.

Finding a dream that is attainable and can one day be realized is strong emotional medicine for those in recovery. It helps them appreciate the need for expanding their clean and sober lifestyle beyond specific recovery accomplishments to spreading their arms to encompass the other riches of life and what life has to offer. It stands to reason that if the alcoholic / addict can funnel their energy toward healthy, productive objectives, they will leave the negative disposition of dry drunk by the wayside and feel fulfilled in a myriad of ways.

9. Plans to make plans:

Thinking their intentions are focused and grounded, alcoholic / addicts might find comfort in making plans just for the sake of making plans. This way they feel that they are moving ahead with their lives, hoping to fulfill a goal that had been percolating for years before a life of addiction took hold. Unfortunately, they can often be all talk and no action.

I believe grunt work and rolling up one's sleeves comes along with trying to realize those goals; it takes commitment and perseverance, something that alcoholic / addicts may have difficulty wrapping their arms around. Fear of failure may stunt their ability to move forward, as there will be many ups and downs before most goals can materialize. Alcoholic / addicts may feel ill-equipped to handle that rollercoaster ride. Or they may believe that they can, but bail at the slightest setback. "Normies," healthy individuals, draw upon their past experiences to learn from mistakes and to not make the same mistake again. However, chances are the alcoholic / addict has been void of those lessons and has to start from the beginning. This can be a daunting and frightening task.

It is hoped that the longer they are in recovery, the more their strength and belief in themselves will grow. Eventually, the lip service of making plans to make plans will be replaced with action. When the action is coupled with consistency, they will experience genuine excitement for the path that lies ahead, including all the successes and failures that go along with the ride. You may grow weary of hearing about your loved one's plans over and over with no action attached. It may be a healthy path for you to ignore or turn a deaf ear to the same dialogue, and in doing so, this might help light a fire under them that springs them into action.

10. Attitude:

Regardless of one's disposition in life, attitude is crucial. You can change your mood or outlook in a split second if you so desire. However, as previously mentioned, the alcoholic/addict may be resentful or angry about having to give up their previous way of life. Their addiction of choice has been their lover, best friend, and companion—and the lifestyle that has gone with it. Hence, their attitude may be poor or questionable from the beginning.

Some people sport a cocky, arrogant attitude and strongly believe that they are better than others in recovery, know more, and can turn their lives around by themselves. Their dogmatic attitude keeps them from acknowledging that they have a lot of work to do and substantial changes to make. This mentality can put them at a disadvantage. The importance of a good attitude and keeping an open mind is paramount when seeking a clean and sober lifestyle. For the alcoholic/addict, a psychological attitude adjustment can start with the word *humble*. When I was a treatment counselor at The Salvation Army, I had my clients look up the word *humble* in the dictionary. After we discussed the definition, I asked them how that state of mind related to them and their recovery; did they see themselves as humble or was there room for improvement?

An interesting and specific example was my client Sam who was in a forced recovery because of a DUI. We spent many sessions talking about his attitude and how he needed to adjust it so that he could accept his sobriety as a newfound freedom instead of a jail sentence. He shared with me that he enjoyed attending A.A. meetings, but only when he felt surrounded by people of his own ilk. If the members didn't share his social or economic status, he would turn a deaf ear to their stories of recovery. This is a perfect example of a much needed attitude adjustment from an inflated ego. With an open mind and good attitude, Sam could have benefited from his meetings, appreciated the commonality, and learned more about himself and his disease. I'm happy to report that after months of attending A.A. meetings, Sam has an excellent attitude, is proud of his open mindedness, and has made some very close friends.

With recovery in particular, changing one's attitude starts with understanding the concept of *being able to ask for help* and realizing that you probably can't lick the addiction on your own. Without starting there, an attitude change can be extremely difficult, and obtaining and accepting the help and viewpoints of others becomes almost impossible. For years, I have understood that one of the main components to a successful Twelve Step recovery program is the ability to share one's experience, strength, and hope—as the programs of both Alcoholics Anonymous and Al-Anon profess.

Jay has attended counseling with me for a few years. He has been very grounded and confident during the six years that he has attended A.A. meetings and shares that he could not do his recovery or remain clean and sober without the help of his fellow alcoholics. Jay shares that when he changed his attitude, became open minded, listened instead of talked, and didn't think he was the authority on everything, then, and only then, could he reap the many benefits that a clean and sober lifestyle had to offer.

When alcoholic / addicts proclaim that they will do whatever it takes to embrace a clean and sober lifestyle, then the road to a better, healthier attitude becomes terra firma under their feet.

11. "Who will I be if I'm not a person addicted to alcohol or other drugs?"

Deciding to become clean and sober can be a very scary endeavor. Undoubtedly, the alcoholic / addict realizes that their life is out of control, and the only way to halt that downward spiral is to change this destructive lifestyle. But fear can often take over—not only fear of the actual physical withdrawal pain but fear of the emotional and psychological pain as well.

Years ago, I was privileged to hear a speaker talk about her fear of the unknown world of sobriety. She was concerned about who and what she would become without alcohol as her constant companion. On top of that, would she even like the new "her" without the crutches of what she had known for so long?

She realized that she had no choice, as the alcoholic in her was going nowhere fast. Sheer desperation pushed her to take the plunge and pray and hope that the landing would be soft. And soft it was. Now she has been clean and sober for many years, married to a terrific man, and enjoying the fruits of motherhood.

I have never met a person in alcohol or drug addiction recovery who is not "happier" leading a clean and sober lifestyle. I also have never met an alcohol-dependent person who did not wish to drink socially and responsibly—like everyone else. They miss their liquid friend as much as they embrace their sobriety. Drug addicts can literally salivate, palpitate, and go into a trance-like state when reliving their love affair with their drug of choice. They, too, realize that life is more fulfilling and satisfying in a myriad of ways because they are leading a clean and sober lifestyle.

Those who are honest about their recovery will gladly tell you that life is substantially better now that they are clean and sober. Though the fear of embracing that sobriety was like a death grip around their throat and a vice around their heart, they powered through and trusted that things would get better. They came to like and respect the new self, and they can now look forward to all that a drug-free/alcohol-free life has to offer.

These are a number of observations I have made over the years as a counselor. Whether working with court-mandated clients or ones freely attending some kind of recovery program, I have found these dispositions and behaviors fairly common among the community of people addicted to alcohol or other drugs. However, addiction is not an exact science, and everyone's recovery is different. Some get clean and sober on their first attempt, while for others it takes years and dozens of relapses. Ultimately, it will be what it will be, as it is all up to the alcoholic / addicts' commitment to their own recovery program.

Sometimes it is necessary to reteach a thing its loveliness ...
until it flowers again from within.
GALWAY KINNELL

Section Two

COMMUNICATION AND BOUNDARIES

The previous section has been all about the characteristics of your loved one—the alcoholic/addict. Now that you are familiar with some of those dispositions, let's turn our attention to you and how you can successfully interact with them and, at the same time, start taking care of yourself. Please keep in mind that though I have broken down these chapters into specifics they all blend together in order to make a complete recovery landscape for you.

Chapter 4

FOLLOW THROUGH WITH YOUR INTENTIONS

It all comes down to credibility—the credibility of the alcoholic/addict as well as your own credibility. If you can't follow through on promises, demands, or consequences then your loved one will know this and learn to exploit it. They will come to understand that your word is built on quicksand and is not to be taken seriously. These are loaded words and probably very confusing as to their meaning other than the obvious. What kind of promises, demands, and all-important consequences are we talking about? In this chapter and subsequent ones, I will explain it in detail, and how it plays out between you and your loved one. These concepts are the backbone of so much interaction between the two of you.

If you don't feel that you can follow through with your intentions and lay out consequences clearly and directly to the alcoholic/addict, then you need to learn how. I know it's scary to hold your ground, but push yourself, and then trust that you are doing the right thing. Remind yourself that there have been too many unsatisfying outcomes or broken promises from your loved one after you both agreed upon different results. In addition, it might help if you can recall how many times you tried and tried various options that did not work, so don't be afraid to try something new.

Discuss small, easy goals that both of you are in agreement with. Make sure they are honest, fair, and well thought out. In doing so, you will be able to stay comfortable and committed—holding your ground if the alcoholic/addict does not keep up their end of the bargain. Remember that this is not a contest to see who will say "uncle" first, to prove who is more stubborn, or to prove that you can go toe-to-toe with them. That motivation (as I'm sure you've experienced on more than one occasion) will only amount to disappointment and wasted energy.

Here's an example of a simple, doable scenario that shouldn't prove to be too much of a white knuckler for you; it is about manners and respect. Say you have told your loved one that if they want to get together for dinner, then a mutually acceptable time needs to be established *and* you expect a clean and sober partner. Once you've agreed on that, state in a quiet, respectful way what the ramifications or consequences will be if either commitment is not met—no fanfare, just business as usual. Do not mention past experiences that have failed. There is no need to say, "Yeah, and you better be there; not like last time when you were two-hours late." IMPORTANT: Before you tell your loved one about these ramifications, make sure that you are 100 percent committed to carrying them out.

If everyone is on board, then continue with an explanation to your loved one that if you don't hear from them or see them by six o'clock (or whatever designated time) that evening, then you will assume that other plans have been made. A phone call at seven o'clock that night with an excuse is unacceptable (unless there's a real emergency), and by then you will have already eaten or made other dinner plans.

In addition, if your loved one comes to dinner in an inebriated or high state, then you calmly share that this behavior is unacceptable, that they have broken the agreement; therefore, the plans for that evening are off. Show your loved one that your actions are speaking as loud as your words by retreating to your room to watch TV or read a book. Or leave the house completely and go to a movie, take a walk, or visit a friend.

Your loved one in recovery may be angry that you have taken this posture (and revert now to punishing you), or they may be relieved to be able to do whatever they want. Chances are that your loved will be confused by your position; realize that holding firm to your commitment is probably new and is causing discomfort to them. You may never have done this before, and when you tried, your loved one knew only too well what buttons to push to make you change your mind.

Your loved one may sulk and pout like a child in the hope of making you feel guilty. This person wants you to overlook that they did not adhere to the plan. *Don't Budge!* You don't have to get angry, be rude, or scold. Just act nonchalant and matter of fact. Show your loved one that you meant what you said, and that in turn, you are taking care of yourself.

This new show of strength is a stepping-stone for both you and your loved one. You are on the road to taking care of yourself with newfound boundaries that spell out self-empowerment and dignity. You are also showing your loved one that you expect behavioral accountability—and that your expectations deserve respect as well.

In time, the confidence you are building with these small goals will prove beneficial for achieving larger ones. Be proud that you have been successful at sticking to your intentions, even though your loved one has not adhered as well as you have. Keep in mind that this exercise is about you, not about them!

Let's look at an example of an intention that might be a bit tougher to implement and which will test your fortitude to follow through. It is hoped that sooner rather than later, you will be comfortable with new challenges such as this one.

For many years I counseled a client who was distressed with her husband's alcoholic propensities and was not shy about letting him know it. He acknowledged her concerns and did his best to cut back. Yet time after time, he always ended up with the same alcohol intake, which led to the same out-of-control behavior. They had planned a camping trip over Thanksgiving. She was anxious about him drinking too much in a place that was desolate, and where she would have no escape if he became too intoxicated. She was tired of waiting to see how far he would go with his drinking and sick of babysitting his inebriated activities.

Together we devised a plan that she would implement if she felt compromised or uncomfortable with the situation. The key to its success was that she felt confident in being able to carry out that plan if necessary.

Before leaving for their camping trip, when he was relaxed and sober, she packed two suitcases and put them by the front door of their home. She informed him that both suitcases were going in the trunk, and that one was for the planned camping trip (which she reiterated that she was looking forward to) and the other was packed with clothes for Palm Springs. Since they had discussed several times how uncomfortable she was with the level of his drinking and his ongoing inability to curb his intake, she calmly stated that if at any time she was feeling anxious about this, she would switch suitcases and head to the desert to have Thanksgiving with friends. Since she would be taking the car, he would be on his own to pack up the gear and somehow get home.

Her husband was stunned at the thought of this scenario, and he displayed a resentful and dour disposition for the next few hours, wondering if he might be left behind. Ultimately, my client reported a wonderful Thanksgiving camping holiday. Though her husband drank, he was respectful of his wife's wishes, and even stated that he enjoyed himself more since he was successful at putting constraints on his alcohol intake.

This represented the beginning of a new level of understanding and communication between the two of them. In addition, on the next several occasions when she discussed her intentions, he knew she would be true to her word, and he respected her more because of it.

Say what you mean and mean what you say! Start small and build upon your victories one intention at a time. After a while it will become like second nature for you, and your loved one will know what the ramifications will be if they don't fulfill their end of the bargain.

The more you practice this resolve and the more successful you become at standing your ground, the more you will find great satisfaction with the empowering feeling that comes from challenging your loved one to respect you and your word.

The greater part of our happiness or misery depends on our dispositions and not on our circumstances.

MARTHA WASHINGTON

Chapter 5

REFUSE TO ENGAGE— TURN A DEAF EAR TO BAITING AND PUNISHMENT

To engage means to participate. Oftentimes, engaging with the alcoholic/addict means that you are paying attention to them and possibly responding with frustration, anger, or negativity. Your loved one has probably gotten used to your engagement. Even when you are screaming at the top of your lungs with no acknowledgment from them, you are engaging and in turn offering attention. Fundamentally, a person with addiction issues would prefer negative attention to no attention at all.

Keep in mind, those who have addiction issues rarely listen past the first sentence, especially if what you are saying is something they don't want to hear. The person will tune you out, walk away, or pretend to oblige just to shut you up. Alcoholic/addicts truly can be masters of selective hearing.

Whether you're talking about addiction or what time to plan for dinner, the alcoholic/addict often lives in their own world, miles away from your world and whatever you're discussing.

Whether your loved one is immersed in addiction or is in recovery, a well meaning, simple discussion sometimes can turn futile. Too often, you can't help but get sucked into a conversation that becomes heated and escalates into a full-blown screaming match. When it gets to that level, no one is listening, and no one can respond with any clear thoughts or act on good intentions. Nothing is accomplished except the building of resentment and anger.

Chances are that both you and your loved one are used to being in each other's faces. Maybe for years this has been the only way that you have communicated, and as a result you are exhausted; it's obviously not working. If you stop arguing, crying, screaming, or jumping out of your skin about this flippant, irresponsible, or questionable behavior, they may become confused or have what I call "a mental short circuit."

Similar to the point made in the previous chapter, not engaging with your loved one will turn out to be very uncomfortable, especially when they are not used to this. You've changed course and gone against the grain of what you both have become used to.

When you calmly disengage from that pattern, be aware that your loved one may fear losing you and wonder, "What happened to my sparring partner?" If you don't engage, your loved one may think that you don't love them anymore. To add to their confusion, your loved one may come to realize that there is no satisfaction in arguing with someone who doesn't argue back. By not engaging, you are in control of your own actions and reactions.

Not engaging also means relaying what you need to say once, maybe twice, with brevity and clarity. Don't let your loved one suck you back into a discussion that you feel you have completed. Debating the issue or questioning your motives are both ways that a person with addiction issues may attempt to keep you engaged.

In addition, by engaging, you may be continuing to fuel the anger against you. It can become a vicious circle—anger keeps the resentment alive, resentment keeps the anger alive. When this state is sustained, your loved one is not capable of focusing on their personal issues. It doesn't take a lot of energy for the alcoholic/addict to stay churned up. The slightest incident can keep their motor running. However, if you don't engage, then your loved one will eventually run out of gas.

Be mindful that even though you may not be verbally engaging, nonverbal communication can result in a locking of horns and be just as powerful. For example, rolling your eyes, crossing your arms, tapping your foot, sighing, or demonstrating blatant indifference can provoke an argument. Speaking to a person sarcastically, whining, mimicking, or using an unpleasant tone or attitude can offer an invitation for engagement even though you haven't raised your voice.

If you are not going to engage with this person, they may turn to plan B—baiting. Don't allow yourself to be roped into moving in this new direction. Baiting and punishing is a method of threatening a family or friend with loaded questions: your loved one wants you to respond a certain way by meeting demands either physically or verbally.

Here are some examples of baiting that the alcoholic / addict may use to engage you in banter:

- "I'm always letting you down."
- "I guess I'm just a bad person."
- "You don't care about me, or you would do this."
- "I can't do anything right."
- "You deserve someone better."
- "You've always liked my sister (or my brother) better than me."
- "You just want to leave me."
- "I don't know why you don't trust me."
- "I guess this is what you want, right?"
- "You have no respect for me."

And my favorite…

- "You just don't love me anymore."

Keep in mind that a loved one with addiction issues is adept in turning the tables back to you. I'm sure you've experienced saying, "You're not being very fair or nice to me," only to hear back, "Well, I don't think you're being very fair or nice to me." This is what I call "boomerang baiting." Your loved one is baiting you for a response, hoping you will engage by defending your position, and working hard to point out what your intentions are. It can be almost impossible to have a reasonable, healthy discussion when the same dialogue goes round and round.

Like in a perfectly staged play, your loved one and you are used to responding with what you have probably said for months, maybe years. Any of the following responses from you will open the door for verbal engagement.

- "Of course not."
- "Don't be silly."
- "That's not true."
- "Okay, what would you like me to do to show you that you're wrong?"
- "No, I never said I wanted that" or "No, let me explain."
- "That's not what my intention was."
- "Why would you think or say that?"

Your objective now is to redirect this routine by responding differently. Don't respond with a question ("Why do you feel that way?"), for the response could be loaded with potential conflict. It also allows the alcoholic / addict to control the response and gives them a sense of power, for you are held captive in waiting for their reply. If you get sucked into answering a question, you may find yourself going round and round, accomplishing nothing. In addition, the answer you give just might come back to bite you one day, as your loved one may unabashedly say, "Well, don't you remember? You told me to do that."

Don't get roped into defending and justifying your position, for more often than not, your loved one is not going to say, "You know you're right; I was wrong" or "I see where you're coming from." Instead, try these responses:

- "I'm sorry you feel that way."
- "I never said that."
- "You must have misheard me."
- "Please don't put words in my mouth."
- "This must be difficult for you."
- "I'm sorry you're sad (or unhappy or lonely or frustrated)."
- "That just won't work for me."
- "It is not healthy for me to participate in this with you."
- Or just walk away calmly, without any discussion, anger, or invoking of your own punishing intentions.

There are two more kinds of baiting that I want to bring to your attention. One is *martyr baiting* and the other is *putting on the charm*. Be aware that if your loved one is unsuccessful in hooking you with some of the bait listed above, they may try to gain a sympathetic engagement by *falling on the sword*. For example, your loved one may state, "That's okay … you've done enough for me already." Or they may say, "Hey, I started this whole mess, why should you expect anything from me?"

A safe answer from you might sound like, "I appreciate your understanding that I can't do that for you anymore." This answer (or one similar) demonstrates not taking the bait, leaving no room for engagement, and staying neutral, yet still being empathetic and loving from a safe distance.

The "putting on the charm" bait can be a way for your loved one to disarm your new impervious skin in an effort to break it down with tactics of charm. "Oh, you look great! How much weight have you lost?" or saying, "You did this or that really well. I'm so impressed with you!" It's hard not to let down your guard and take the bait when one is dripping with honey compliments. Don't be taken for a momentary ride.

If you don't take the bait, your loved one has nowhere to go. We all have buttons that when pushed elicit a sometimes less than favorable or immature response. If this person with addiction issues is an intimate part of your life, they will know what sets you off and what is an especially sensitive area for you. You find yourself defending and protecting who you are, and while doing so, you are engaging in a heated, pointless, and fruitless discussion that will lead nowhere. Your loved one will remember this engagement for a nanosecond, but you on the other hand, might have your day ruined.

Be mindful that your loved one may attempt to bait and then engage you from old conversations. For example, if you once confessed that you felt that you were not a particularly attentive mother, don't allow your loved one to have a field day during an argument by bringing up your weakness and sandbagging you. Your faults or flaws (and everyone has them) do not make you an uncaring parent, an unloving and insensitive mate, or a bad friend to others. You don't need to defend yourself, as it is a waste of time; frankly, it should be below your dignity. However, the lesson to be learned is that sometimes innocent comments made to your loved one, or discussions you have together, can be turned against you in the form of pot shots at your emotional fiber.

Be careful of hooks, baits, and set-ups. If you can be successful in keeping a watchful eye for them, then you will be well prepared to hit the nonengagement brake each and every time.

You don't have to suffer continual chaos in order to grow.
JOHN C. LILLY

Chapter 6

STAY NEUTRAL

A car that is in neutral doesn't go anywhere, neither forward nor backward. Staying neutral with your loved one means offering no opinion one way or the other. It means finding that middle ground and neither validating nor challenging what he or she is communicating to you.

Staying neutral is safe. No one can come back and blame you for saying this or that. No one will attack you for encouraging an action or specific behavior. When you stay neutral, you turn decisions over to the alcoholic / addict to make independently; you are empowering this person with the capacity to make choices, and at the same time, you are empowering yourself with a commitment to neutrality. Your loved one will be afforded the opportunity to learn from their own decision, not yours. That decision may garner positive results or not, but either way the alcoholic / addict will be in charge of the outcome, not you.

Staying neutral and "refusing to engage" (chapter 5) are two strategies that must be employed simultaneously. One cannot be totally effective without the other. If you are successful in implementing both of these concepts, I promise that you will feel more grounded and confident, with renewed self-respect and dignity about your interactions. Your relationship with your loved one will take on a new dimension because you have "short circuited" this habitual thinking by responding differently than on previous occasions.

Staying neutral is not easy. Your loved one is asking your opinion or seeking your advice, and you want so desperately to give them the benefit of your knowledge. You can't help but think that maybe you will present something or unlock the door to what might be the answer that you both have waited years to find. If you really feel compelled to voice your opinion, then first determine if your loved one genuinely and honestly wants your input; the best time is when they are calm, making eye contact, and engaged in a positive, nonagitated way. Mirror these dispositions so everyone is communicating on a level playing field. If you are not comfortable giving advice, for you feel it may blow up in your face, use specific words to stay neutral. I have compiled some detached and safe responses for you to consider:

- "You've asked for my opinion, but it may not be what you want to hear."
- "I don't know enough about the situation."
- "I don't have enough facts to make a comfortable assessment."
- "Use your own best judgment."
- "That's up to you."
- "I think I'm too close to the situation to give an unbiased opinion."
- "You seem to have given this enough thought to make a decision."
- "I really have no opinion one way or the other."
- "I'm uncomfortable getting in the middle of this."
- "I've addressed this issue before, and you know how I feel."

As previously stated, you must remember that not only the words that come out of your mouth need to be neutral, but also your tone, attitude, and expressions need to follow suit. If you say, "Use your own best judgment," with a "You really are an idiot" or "That's the dumbest thing I've ever heard" inflection in your voice, you will become ineffective. That tone will trump the neutrality of your position.

Let's look at more specific examples of staying neutral where a more complete response is necessary to end a discussion or deal with your own unfinished business.

Here is a letter that my client Gloria and I wrote, as she needed to implement neutrality and establish new boundaries in dealing with her alcohol-dependent father.

Dear Dad,

It has been a few months since our last visit. I have spent some time thinking about you and where we stand in our relationship. I love you, Dad, but my thoughts are torn between allowing myself to be available to you (and your out-of-control behavior) and my taking care of my family and myself.

Currently I am sad, confused, angry, and, frankly, frightened. I'm sure your intentions are not to have me feel this way, but I do, nonetheless.

With that said, I have carefully put together some boundaries that I think will help both of us enjoy a more respectful and healthy relationship.

- No one can be around my family under the influence of drugs or alcohol. If I feel uncomfortable, I will leave and take the boys.
- I won't respond to your calls threatening suicide. If you call me, I will call the police and ask them to take over. I can't be of any service to you, as I am not a trained professional in the area of suicide.
- I no longer will help you if you are arrested for any incident or are in legal trouble. Again, I am not a trained professional in the area of legal matters.
- I am uncomfortable when you argue with Ellen in front of the children and me. If you do, and my family or I feel compromised, I will quietly leave.

I hope you can understand and respect my wishes. My plate is full with my career, my husband, and my two young boys who have developmental challenges; I neither have the time nor energy to have my father as a burden instead of a joy.

I will wait for your response.

Much love,
Gloria

This letter is loving, yet strong and determined in posture. Gloria can feel good that she is being true to herself and getting her point across while staying neutral.

Here is an example of role-playing that my client Annie and I went through regarding her communication with her daughter. Annie's daughter is in her mid-twenties, and sadly, Annie has painfully allowed her daughter to bully and verbally abuse her. Annie needed guidance in staying neutral with her communication as her daughter tried desperately to bait and hook her. I have listed fifteen role-plays of actual dialogue from her daughter and the responses I guided Annie with in return. Keep in mind that Annie was totally fed up with her daughter's disrespect and lack of fair communication skills for years, so you may view these responses as too harsh or uncaring, but they were perfect for her.

Daughter: "I can't believe you are not going to give me money when I can't even afford to get something to eat."
Annie: "I will be happy to take you to lunch, and there's plenty of food at home if you're strapped right now and can't afford to go out and eat."

Daughter: "I can't believe that you won't pay to take Gizmo to the vet. I thought you loved him. He is coughing and could be dying."
Annie: "Poor Gizmo. This must be hard for you to watch your pet in pain. Maybe you can drive him to a clinic and ask for a payment plan, or tell them you can help by dog walking or cleaning out the cages as a way of barter."

Daughter: "I can't believe you won't pay to keep my car from being shut-off. If it's shut off, I can't go look for a job or work."
Annie: "Sorry, your car is your responsibility. People do get around by walking, biking, or taking a bus. Another option is that you might have to find a job close to home where you won't have to drive. It's unfortunate that the only way you could get a car was with a shut-off device installed for when you didn't pay on time; that must be frustrating."

Daughter: "I can't believe you won't give me cash so I can start doing things with friends and get my life back."
Annie: "I think it's great that you want to re-establish your relationships with your friends, but I'm confused as to how this affects me."

Daughter: "I can't believe you won't give me money for work clothes. I can't earn any money without work clothes."

Annie: "Okay, I'll take you shopping, and I'm willing to lay out $75.00 for work clothes. However, I will expect to be reimbursed in full by your third paycheck."

Daughter: "My roommate can't believe how selfish you are being about giving me any money. Now I'm going to have to borrow from him or my previous drug dealer. Then I'll have to do things to pay him off that won't be nice, and I might start using again."

Annie: "Yikes! What a scary thought, but you obviously need to do what you need to do. It's a good thing that you are an adult and responsible for your own actions."

Daughter: "So you're okay with not supporting me and that it might get me to start using drugs and alcohol or try suicide again. You're really willing to do that and take that chance?"

Annie: "It certainly makes me sad to think that you might start using drugs again or even kill yourself. But, I have been down this road before with you, and I can't do it again. I will pray that you will find a solution to your situation that's not so dramatic ... and final."

Daughter: "I can't believe that you will turn your phones off at night. It's later here, and I may need to talk to you in the morning. It may be an emergency, and I might need to be able to reach you."

Annie: "When you become more responsible and respectful about calling me and being considerate of my time, then maybe I won't turn the phone off. Until then, you are just a crank caller, and I don't have the time or energy to pick up the phone only to hang it up. I'm sure whatever it is can most likely wait until the morning."

Daughter: "I don't understand why I am not important to you anymore since I left California. I need to have someone to talk to, and you are the only one that I can depend on. So you need to take my calls."

Annie: "I'm more than happy to take your calls and be there for you. However, we need some new boundaries. You can call twice a day at _____ and _____. Not only will I not be available to you more than that, but if you don't respect these guidelines, the calls will be reduced to once a day and then none for that day. Conversely, if you adhere to our agreement, I'll add one additional call sometime over the weekend when I have time."

Daughter: "So you're going to hang up the phone when I'm upset. You call yourself part of my family. You are the crappiest mother anyone could have. What mother acts like that to her only child?"

Annie: "I will not allow you or anyone to talk with disrespect or a belligerent attitude or tone to me. I don't deserve it, and I don't care what you think of me as a mother. Respect is earned and should be mutual. If it's not there, then I am not interested in any communication whatsoever. And, the next time you use profanity toward me or scream at me, I will not take your calls until you have sent me a written apology. I won't allow myself to be bullied by your out-of-control behavior just to perpetuate your grandstanding."

Daughter: "Everything is going so bad. I can't get a job, you won't help me, and I'm tired of trying. I just want to not wake up tomorrow; it's just not worth it anymore."

Annie: "I'm sorry you feel so dejected. I'm sure you'll find a solution, as you are such a smart, resourceful young lady."

Daughter: "I don't have any friends and can't see that changing. I don't want to live like this anymore."

Annie: "I'm sorry you're feeling this way. It must be difficult to not have any friends. However, I'm confident that you will find your way out of this."

Daughter: "So you won't give me any more money. So you

want me to become a stripper or pimp myself out. Would that make you happy since you won't help me?"

Annie: "If that's what you feel your only options are for making money, then that's what you'll have to do." I guess you know your capabilities, and if stripping or prostitution is how you see your career then you should follow that path.""

Daughter: "So you'll only give me grocery and gas cards. So you don't trust me with money?"

Annie: "I think I'm being generous by gifting you money for groceries and gas. I'm sorry that you don't like the way it's being offered to you. I think it might be a good idea if I stopped doing anything financial; you are obviously not happy with the arrangement, and your level of gratitude is below sea level. Yes, no more cards for grocery or gas until your attitude has a substantial adjustment. Trying to win through intimidation is growing very thin and weary for me."

Daughter: "So you say your marriage will be affected if you give me more money. So it's okay for me to starve while you and your husband sit in your nice house in California and have a good life?"

Annie: "Not that I owe you an explanation, but my husband and I have worked hard to enjoy our nice house in California. And frankly, it's none of your business how we spend our money, or where we spend our money. It is, after all, our money to spend."

I cannot stress enough how important a neutral posture is. Your loved one wants you to be as accountable as they are, a partner in crime. If you stay neutral (and do not engage), you are affording a way for them to form personal decisions, and you are posturing to them to be accountable.

When new clients come to me, I tell them that the most important things to implement are to *refuse to engage* and to *stay neutral!* I strongly suggest that they write those two phrases down on dozens of sticky notes and place them everywhere so that they can see them constantly. Put them on the steering wheel, inside a wallet, on the refrigerator door, next to the telephone—anywhere that will be a visual reminder and mental exercise. It is okay if your loved one sees this. This can turn out to be a good and productive way for the other person to see that you are starting to take care of yourself by implementing new tools and communication techniques.

Nothing can bring you peace but yourself.

RALPH WALDO EMERSON

Chapter 7

BREATHE AND HIT PAUSE— THINK TWICE, ACT ONCE

All of us have knee-jerk reactions to things that push our buttons, and some of us can go from zero to sixty faster than others. Many feel that if they don't retaliate immediately, either with words or actions, then it's a sign of weakness. Getting angry too often can be like crying wolf: no one will believe that you are justified in your anger if you get worked up too frequently.

Those few precious seconds, minutes, or hours where you breathe and hit the pause button might allow you to think twice and act once. It will give you time to regroup and respond thoughtfully rather than have a harsh reaction or emotion—and one that you might regret later. Most likely, after years of manipulative conversations and actions with your loved ones, they know what kind of response they will evoke in you. If you pause, stay neutral, and don't engage, then you can put yourself in control. Don't hand the baton over to the person with addiction issues to conduct the exchange.

Hitting the pause button allows you to take stock of the situation before acting on it impetuously, allowing you time to calculate your next action so you can come from a place of confidence and stability rather than emotion and passion. It also demonstrates restraint and maturity and will signify to the alcoholic / addict that they do not have the power to get your goat.

As I've stated previously, maintaining silence (silence can be a very powerful response) or a passive stance can be unnerving and uncomfortable to the alcoholic/addict because they are not used to, and may be anxious about, what is coming next.

Changing the routine from what it once was will show your loved one that you are starting to map out a firm attitude of your own—becoming more resilient to their behavior.

Though this concept seems simple on the surface, it can be challenging to implement. Your knee-jerk reaction might not be an angry response to something, but about wanting to jump right in to protect your loved one from making bad decisions or using poor judgment. You may feel that if you don't respond immediately, then you may lose the momentum of the moment or the opportunity to come up with the perfect answer. If you are able to hit the pause button, you will give yourself a chance to curb your instinct to rescue, enable, or provide your loved one with a solution that would prove more beneficial if they came up with it on their own.

So, you've successfully hit the pause button, but you still want to say or do something. Before acting, consider these three groups of questions to make sure that you are clear on your intentions:

1. What's the point? Will it change anything? Have I considered the source?
2. Will I be okay with the outcome? Is it okay if a friendship or employment ends?
3. How important is it? Is it really worth me saying something?

Hitting the pause button is a healthy exercise and an important habit to master. You may find it beneficial with relationships other than with the alcoholic/addict. Consider all options carefully, and try as best you can to assess the different possibilities of your outcome before opening your mouth, even if the intentions come from your heart.

Patience is the key to paradise.

TURKISH PROVERB

Chapter 8

PAY ATTENTION TO YOUR COMMUNICATION

One of the most difficult tasks is learning to communicate effectively with the alcoholic/addict. You may have every intention of not engaging and staying neutral, but often that falls apart as your loved one can deftly twist and turn your comments to satisfy their desires—until you become exhausted and end up acquiescing, making excuses, or even apologizing. Here are some thoughts to ponder when having a dialogue with the alcoholic/addict.

Turn the Question Back on Them

One simple concept that might help set a steadier verbal course is to turn questions or statements back onto your loved one. For example, if you're asked how you think they are doing in school, work, relationships, recovery, or anything else for that matter, consider this response, "How do *you* think you're doing?" or confirm, "You must feel good about what you're accomplishing." Though validation is nice, your answer is not really important because it is about how the alcoholic/addict believes they are doing.

The alcoholic/addict may be looking for a genuine response from you, but be aware that this could also be an invitation for engagement or a way to exploit you further down the road. This may come back in the form of, "Well, you told me to do this" or "You told me to say that." Don't relinquish your opinion so freely. You can still communicate, but let your loved one answer their questions first before you so eagerly present yours.

By doing so, you will be able to gauge where your loved one is coming from through tone and attitude.

Use Nonaggressive Words or Phrases

Why give your loved one any reason to be combative, defensive, or in your face? Try not to start a sentence with "Why" (as in "Why didn't you do this?" or "Why did you say that?"), for it is accusatory and could invite a combative response.

One way to avoid conflict is to indemnify yourself before speaking or make a concession statement even if you don't think one is needed or appropriate. When using this technique, and in general when communicating, use "I" statements often. For example, "I might not know what I'm talking about, but ..." or "I may be totally wrong in my perception, but ..."

If you immediately take responsibility for the degree to which you are uninformed, you present your vulnerability. When this occurs, it might be harder for the alcoholic/addict to come back with something other than a calm demeanor. Your loved one may become frustrated because you are not giving them the answer they want, or the answer that they have been used to hearing. In addition, if you don't respond with aggression, they may have a difficult time feeling justified in their anger if anger is percolating under the surface. The combination of not engaging (chapter 5), neutrality (chapter 6), and self-indemnification can be very powerful in the world of communicating with the alcoholic/addict.

Here are some words and phrases that are nonaggressive, yet can be empowering when used calmly and with confidence:

PROCESS

This is a great word that is more descriptive than *think*. The alcoholic/addict may want something from you, and instead of the generic answer that you "want to think about it," try saying, "I need to process this." This packs a more intellectual punch and signifies that you intend to really analyze the situation more than you might normally. The phrase *let me think about it,* which is a normal, typical response, signifies somewhat of a power trip on your end. It has an underlying implication that says if they are "good," chances are they will receive a positive response. Saying that you want to "process" your thoughts has nothing to do with granting a request. Its meaning is direct. By processing, you are saying that you will be taking many things into consideration and weighing different options to help you make a decision that *you* are comfortable with, even though they may not be. Also, there is no need to respond to your loved one too quickly. Take your time; even if you have already processed your answer, let them wait. After all, your loved one's life has been about so much instant gratification, either with satisfying their addiction or getting attention from family members or friends. It might be good for them to learn a bit of patience and to cool their heels and wait for someone else for a change.

COMFORTABLE/UNCOMFORTABLE

Both are descriptive words that have a sense of visualization attached to them. For example, "I'm uncomfortable with your plan," sounds better than, "I don't like your plan." Stating that you don't like something is strong and critical and can be taken as a challenge. The alcoholic / addict may start to defend or justify their reasoning. Conversely, stating your "comfort," as in "I'm comfortable with that idea" can be construed as positive reinforcement. It is also more thoughtful than, "That's fine," "That's good," or "That's okay with me," which can sound passive-aggressive.

Personally and professionally, I love the words *comfortable* and *uncomfortable*. People don't like to think or know that someone they care about is uncomfortable. It is a bit of a rescue word, and one that brings forth an image of enveloping someone in security and warmth. It is difficult to get angry, resentful, or combative with someone who is honest at admitting to a level of discomfort about something or acknowledging feelings.

SAD/SADDENED

These words are descriptive and softly visual. For example, "It makes me sad when you engage in reckless behavior" or "I'm saddened by the way you treat me when you are drunk or high." These words should replace, "I'm angry," "I'm annoyed," and "I don't like." I have found that when family members or friends say to someone that they are sad when being shouted at, embarrassed, or disrespected, then the person may be resentful initially at being called out on the carpet for their actions, but the alcoholic / addict is ultimately ashamed of this behavior and becomes saddened as well, knowing that loved ones feel this way. I believe that these words inspire empathy rather than defensiveness.

DISAPPOINTED

This is a tricky word. If not used properly, it can be taken as a scolding or admonishment. However, using it the right way, "I'm not going to lie to you. I'm disappointed in your decision" (or behavior or failure to do this or that) or even, "You must be disappointed in the outcome," allows you to stay neutral and not engage. You may be madder than a hornet, but using the word *disappointed* diffuses the issue and allows you to still be honest about what you are feeling. Using it the wrong way, "Well, once again, you've disappointed me (or everyone), and I (we) shouldn't expect anything different, so what else is new," has you engaging with your admonishment. The response you will likely get from your loved one will either be, "I'm nothing but a loser" or "Who cares what you think, bite me!" This will be a lose/lose situation all around. Disappointment is a combination of a state of mind and an emotion, as opposed to expressing anger, which can be explosive but subsides with time.

CONFUSED

This is one of my favorite words. For example, using the word *confused* as in, "I'm sorry, I'm confused. I thought you told me that you were going to do this," puts the responsibility back on your loved one to explain their actions.

Your loved one may get flustered when answering or give you double-talk, since you might have caught them in a lie. The bottom line is about calling one's bluff. You know your loved one has not kept their word, and they know that as well. Be careful not to fall prey to a list of excuses. There is nothing wrong with pressing someone for a new game plan under the guise that you want to avoid ongoing confusion.

Try to stay away from using words like *good, bad, right,* or *wrong*. They are hard to define, and their generic meaning makes them too judgmental. They also work against staying neutral and not engaging.

Let's not forget that "No" is a complete sentence. You can certainly ask what part of "No" they don't understand, but any elaboration is probably wasted energy, and that is an open door for engagement and non-neutrality.

Here are some other words that are more creative and show thought in communicating:

- CHALLENGE: "I'm confident that you can meet this challenge. You're smart and capable."
- UNCERTAIN: "I'm uncertain where you are headed with this. Would you please explain it to me?"

- PLEASED: "I'm so pleased that you decided to do this (or do that)." "You must be pleased as well with your decision."
- GROUNDED: "Your plan sounds very grounded and well thought through."
- FOCUSED: "I'm glad to see you're so focused with your goal."
- EMPATHETIC: "I'm empathetic with your struggle (disappointment/frustration)." (Substitute whatever emotion your loved one is undergoing at that time.)

Here are some additional phrases that might help you with calmer communication:

- "This is where I'm coming from … "
- "This is how I'm feeling … "
- "This is what is making me a little anxious … "
- "Please help me to understand … "
- "I'm sorry, but I'm struggling with … "
- "Let me repeat this, so I know I'm clear … "

None of these words or phrases listed above should provoke a fight. If you think one is starting because your loved one wants you to use your old words or terminology, back away calmly and without anger.

Your goal with all of these concepts should be to re-establish your own self-respect and dignity as you learn new communication skills. Your loved one will have no choice but to either participate the way you want or not at all. You are not punishing them, merely moving new communication pieces around the board.

If you can learn these key words and phrases as a second language, your communication will be less volatile and hopefully more productive.

I now choose to rise above my personality problems to recognize the magnificence of my being. I am totally willing to learn to love myself.

LOUISE L. HAY

Chapter 9

ARE YOUR EXPECTATIONS DANGEROUS?—KEEPING THINGS IN PERSPECTIVE

I have come to believe that the word *expectations* can be one of the dirtiest words in the English language. When dealing in the world of addiction, more often than not, expectations are rarely realized.

We have heard sayings like, *Don't set your expectations too high* or *Curb your expectations*. Try as you might, you can't help but to dream, plot, or plan out calculated moves in order for your expectations to come to fruition. Most people have a tough enough time trying to control their expectations in regard to their own daily life. Pinning those invisible and emotional expectations on your loved one, more often than not, is destined for failure.

You need to be bold enough and strong enough to let your loved one's recovery unfold or not unfold as it is meant to, not as *you* want it to. This is an important start in reining in your expectations, and by doing so you will be ahead of the curve. Your expectations should not be part of your loved one's life. Even if they are enrolled in the best rehabilitation program in the world, remember that it is not your program; your expectations should not be hanging onto your loved one's performance or success.

Even with the best intentions toward recovery, the alcoholic / addict may have a relapse or two. If you believe otherwise, not only will your expectations go unfulfilled or even be shattered, but also your loved one may be doubly distressed either by not meeting their own expectations and/or not meeting yours.

It will likely help with your expectations if you understand that this disease is a chronic battle. Addiction is never cured, merely arrested. That said, like any disease, it is also harder to understand this when you don't have the disease.

If your expectations are not met, it may be difficult to cover up your disappointment. It is possible that your loved one will sense this and realize that they are the reason for your sorrow. If your loved one starts to lose faith as well, this may create added pressure and possibly fuel a downward spiral. Your loved one may think, "What difference does it make?" "I can't do anything right. Once again, I have failed my family and friends by not satisfying their expectations or mine."

These pointers will help you manage your expectations:

Keep things in perspective. For example, if your loved one is coming out of a residential rehabilitation program, chances are that the program was only for thirty or sixty days. Most rehabilitation programs will offer some kind of after care, such as a sober living house or continued care at their facility, but with fewer restrictions.

It is understandable that you and everyone else are thrilled when your loved one has been clean and sober for more days than maybe any previous efforts. They look healthy, talk with confidence, and are really feeling good about themselves and the experience they have just gone through. Everyone should be proud, but please remember that those thirty, sixty, or even ninety days are only the beginning of an arduous journey. The alcoholic/addict has been clean and sober for the width of an eyelash compared to the possibly *years* of addiction. You do the math—it will probably take more than a few months to become confident and assured about living a clean and sober lifestyle. You may know this instinctively, but don't think that whatever number of days spent in treatment will produce a cure—no matter what your loved one says or how they act or look. All that has been accomplished is the detoxification stage, and the alcoholic/addict is only just starting to understand, realize, and appreciate how good life can be when leading a clean and sober lifestyle. There is a lot of hard work ahead in dealing with all the emotional and psychological baggage that brought your loved one to the addiction in the first place. Both you and your loved one should keep a tight grip on your expectations regarding the long road ahead when starting to re-enter a healthy world of living. Being physically clean and sober is very different than being emotionally and psychologically clean and sober.

In addition, be honest with yourself about what your loved one can and cannot accomplish. Even clean and sober, your loved one may not be capable of certain tasks or assignments. At one time, the addiction might have been an excuse for laziness or zero motivation. Just because the alcoholic / addict has embraced a clean and sober lifestyle, they may not have the disposition or even the desire to change what was once known and was comfortable to them.

It is hoped that the person in addiction recovery has expectations as well. If the expectations are unrealistic, then they may not know how to handle the disappointment because of an unsatisfactory outcome. Furthermore, if your expectations run a parallel course, then you both will go round and round—losing sight of what's realistic and doable. Don't let your expectations bring your loved one to a place where they cannot be successful. Let them lead the way, for their expectations of themselves may be totally different than what you have in mind.

Keep your expectations in close check. No need to voice them; just hope to be pleasantly surprised if they come to pass. If they don't, you can be disappointed, but it will serve no purpose to share this with the alcoholic / addict.

Don't be overzealous about small victories nor nonchalant about larger accomplishments. I believe the more you can keep things on an even keel and stop looking at your loved one as though they live in a fish bowl, the more relaxed, understanding, and patient everyone involved can be. Your loved one is not a baby. When a baby takes their first step you jump for joy and call everyone you know. But too much fanfare for tasks that should be standard operating procedure can be embarrassing to the alcoholic / addict, and they may find themselves feeling uncomfortable with your over-the-top attention. If you feel you want to acknowledge something that they did, then make a special dinner, take them to a movie or fill their car with gas. A quiet pat on the back can be very gratifying.

Conversely, if the alcoholic / addict has landed a job, been accepted to college, or celebrates a milestone of sobriety (these situations could not have happened if your loved one was not practicing a clean and sober lifestyle), then a good, healthy celebration is in order. After all, you might do that for anyone regardless of an addiction issue. I will talk more about the rewards for good behavior in a later chapter.

One last thought: you may be tempted to voice a recovery victory and expectations to your friends and family. It's exciting news that your loved one may finally be on a healthy path. However, when you talk about them, try to stay away from saying, "She is doing great" or "Everything is fine and back to normal." Your expectations (and those of your loved one) will be better served if instead you say, "He seems grounded," "She seems focused on recovery," or "He seems committed to his recovery." You can only speak for the moment, and this is a good habit for you to practice. Words like *great, fine,* and *normal* can be vague in their definition, and the bar for success for these words can be very lofty. In addition, you have now included others to carry around the same expectations as you have, and it can be a pretty heavy bundle and one that is difficult to unload if expectations are not kept up.

Change your thoughts and you change your world.
NORMAN VINCENT PEALE

Chapter 10

SHED YOUR SKIN OF ENABLING AND RESCUING

"I was terribly confused about the meaning of *compassion* when I came to Al-Anon. I thought it meant making excuses for the alcoholic/addict or covering their bad checks. Al-Anon helped me to find another word for this behavior: *enabling*. I learned that when I cleaned up the consequences of their behavior, I enabled the person to continue drinking comfortably and acting out without having to pay the price. A more compassionate way to respond to those I love might be to allow them to face the consequences of their actions, even when it will cause them pain."[6]

This is quoted from the Al-Anon book *Courage to Change,* and truer words have never been spoken. But what do they mean? Who is the "enabler"? What does the "rescuer" look like, and why are these labels so apt for so many well-meaning people?

As caring, compassionate people, we naturally and instinctively want to protect and help our loved ones. There is a universal urge in both animals and human beings to protect those that may be heading for a potentially harmful situation. We must learn to work at being part of the solution, not the problem.

Liz is a client who came to me exhausted, knowing that she was constantly enabling and rescuing her thirty-six-year-old daughter. Her daughter had moved three times from the Midwest to California. If Liz heard only a whimper from her daughter expressing trepidation about traveling alone, Liz would drive her car or hop on a plane to "help" her daughter drive the 2,500 miles to the West Coast. When I asked Liz about this, I learned that the leash she felt her daughter had on her embarrassed her. However, in the same breath, she justified her actions by saying that her daughter had a horrible sense of direction, would probably get lost, and possibly be in danger.

Liz's answer should have been to rent her daughter a GPS system, have her fly, or take a bus or train. The solution was not for Liz to drop everything and swoop down to rescue her daughter, but to find a more logical and healthy way for her daughter to overcome her neediness.

Enabling and rescuing makes us feel wanted and needed. It is a momentary adrenaline rush—when for a brief instant we are the savior and the center of someone else's world. The alcoholic / addict thanks us and is grateful, and since it is likely that someone else has said "no" to him or her, you become the *hero du jour* ... and that is a heck of a warm and fuzzy feeling. The addiction (yes, I said *addiction*) of enabling and rescuing others over and over again can be enticing to people who don't have much going on in their own personal life or people who generally feel unfulfilled.

Some people find great satisfaction in wearing the enabling-and-rescuing crown. If someone is unfulfilled in their own personal life, it is simple to ease that bland disposition by suggesting or foisting an opinion or even by taking over another's life based on the belief that they don't think they are doing a good enough job. Under the guise of not approving of the lifestyle the other is leading, this can be a fertile ground for enabling and rescuing.

People who need attention or validation of their existence may be seeking the attention of others to satisfy these needs. A wonderful way to satisfy that need is for one to enable and rescue another who is perceived to be screaming out for a life preserver, whether the individual actually is or not. Enablers think they know best. By donning a rescue cape, the hope is that the rescuer will be praised for the efforts, insights, and sensitivity, and also that, when all is said and done, the rescuer can take a well-deserved bow for having a sixth sense and saving the day.

Remember that sometimes enabling and rescuing can backfire into a situation that is worse than it was before these so called noble attempts. Unintentionally, you may be prolonging someone who is in need of a recovery program, or even worse endangering their well being by falling for their pleas for money or prescription medication.

Here is an example of someone with good intentions of wanting to help another but instead enables and rescues them to satisfy their own personal needs; consequently, they are blind to the detrimental outcome.

My client Claire has a daughter who was lost in life and using illicit substances. Claire had a good relationship with her brother, though the relationship was volatile at times, as they both have strong personalities and are very opinionated. Claire's brother had no natural children (though his wife had two from a previous marriage), and he wanted very much to participate in the lives of Claire's children.

Claire had a very challenging and difficult relationship with her daughter, Tricia, who was struggling with addiction issues and eating disorders. Claire was making an effort to abstain from enabling and rescuing and was working toward a partnership with mutually agreed upon goals and guidelines regarding Tricia's life choices.

Tricia wanted to change locales and lifestyles her way and would not entertain any of Claire's suggestions regarding putting a plan together for work, school, or expenses. Tricia went behind Claire's back to her uncle and found success with Mr. Enabler-Rescuer. He sent money for Tricia to move, and then set her up in an apartment with the requirements being that she would get a job or go to school, and of course, remain clean and sober. Because of Tricia's life of addiction, she was unable to succeed in any of these demands. Claire's brother felt he could not abandon her, so he found himself knee deep in seeking rehabilitation and recovery programs for her, which was a foreign world to him.

It took some time for resentment to subside, as Claire was angry with her brother's meddling in an area he knew nothing about. She appreciated the love he had shown Tricia, but rescuing her with no foundation or knowledge as to how serious her issues were, or what would be healthy alternatives, proved to be a plan of poor judgment and not in Tricia's best interest.

Though difficult to accept, ego and love can sometimes blind you from making the right and wise decision to disengage. Step aside, and let a professional advise you on the situation. Don't let that ego get in the way of you keeping an open and honest mind in finding the proper solution.

In chapter 3, I talk about the alcoholic/addict who might wish to pick and choose their recovery process. The same is true for the enabling and rescuing friend or family member who doesn't want to get involved in certain parts of rescuing and enabling, but who wants to lead the brigade in other parts.

George came to me for clarification regarding his daughter's addiction and how she had been MIA for several months. George had asked his daughter to leave the family home if she could not sustain a clean and sober lifestyle. One day, George received a phone call that his daughter was in jail. He professed that he hoped this was his daughter's wake-up call for sobriety, and he committed himself to remain on the sidelines and watch the play unfold. Since he had been down this road of recovery and relapse before, he was not going to let himself become enmeshed as he had in the past. However, George stated that he would find the best lawyer money could buy if he felt his daughter wasn't going to get a fair shake with the legal system.

I would categorize this as picking and choosing one's enabling and rescuing, much like the alcoholic/addict may pick and choose which parts of their recovery they want to participate in and which parts they want nothing to do with.

As difficult as this may be to witness, events need to unfold on their own accord. If enabled or rescued, the alcoholic/addict is prevented from experiencing actions due to their decisions or that are derived from irresponsible or out-of-control behavior.

Enabling and rescuing can be dangerous; what you think might be a lifeline could result in a precarious outcome for the alcoholic/addict. Whether you think you know or whether you have no clue about the person's patterns regarding addiction, innocent, well intended enabling or rescuing could promote more destructive behavior. Here is a list of fifteen reasons why we continue to rescue and enable even though we know we should turn and walk away:

1. We hope against all hope that tomorrow will be different, so we try yet again.
2. Ego—we are the ones that save the day.
3. Ego again—we have a desire to be liked, appreciated, or held in high esteem
4. We think, "What if our loved one dies and we could have prevented it, or worse that we are responsible?"
5. We don't want to hurt our loved one's feelings by saying "no."
6. We fear our loved one's anger and the risk of punishment or retribution.
7. We are afraid the person addicted to alcohol or other drugs may do something "bad" (act out) and blame us for the destructive actions. (This is an "I'll show you" or "You'll be sorry" posture.)

8. We believe that our loved one is sick and not responsible for these behaviors.

9. We believe that the problems of the alcoholic / addicts are our fault, so how can we not help them?

10. We fear that family members, or friends will think poorly of us, or they'll think of us as a person who doesn't care about our own loved ones.

11. The alcoholic / addict has presented something different, a new plan for their recovery, so we climb on board one more time.

12. We are too weary or even lazy to implement change. We think, "What's the point?"

13. This "dance" has been part of our lives for so long; we don't know what purpose we would have without it.

14. We are embarrassed and want to protect other family members.

15. We are embarrassed and want to protect ourselves.

We all fall into some of these categories during different times of our lives, but it is hoped that these behaviors cease after they run their course, and after we realize that rescuing is fruitless and doesn't help the alcoholic / addict one bit toward taking appropriate responsibility for their actions. It takes strength, confidence, and fortitude to not be tempted to enable or rescue. But, please work at it; it is truly the healthy path for both you and your loved one.

Help them to take failure, not as a measure of their worth,
but as a chance for a new start.

BOOK OF COMMON PRAYER

Chapter 11

DON'T QUIZ OR MONITOR THE ALCOHOLIC / ADDICT'S PROGRESS OR LACK OF IT

Let's assume that the person in your life with an addiction has finally decided to head down the path of recovery. They have come to the realization that their life is in a nosedive due to addiction and out-of-control behavior. Maybe your loved one has hit bottom because of infractions with the law, losing a job, or worst of all, alienation from family and home. Whatever the reason, this person has decided to get help.

As loving and supportive family members and friends, our first inclinations might be to roll up our sleeves and immerse ourselves in their recovery program. Although it is difficult to step back, family members and friends must do so, as these are *their* decisions and these are *their* programs—not yours. Whether they fail or succeed, they need to map out their plans *their* way not your way. Family members and friends must be in the cheering section in the bleachers, not the coaches running the playbooks on the field.

Here are seven reasons why your involvement is not constructive or healthy for either the alcoholic / addict or you:

1. Unless we are sitting right next to the person at a Twelve Step meeting, outpatient rehabilitation program, or counseling session, you have no idea if your loved one has even attended the meetings or sessions. The person with addiction issues may stay for fifteen minutes or walk in the front door and right out the back.

89

Even when asked, they may not tell the truth.

2. Although it sounds harsh, what the alcoholic/addict does is *none of our business* They may start out with good intentions and continue on that road, or they may start to sputter before they can get a solid handle on what their recovery looks like or should be. Whatever they do, it has to be their journey, for no one is standing in their shoes but them.

3. Monitoring or quizzing may be construed as not trusting or checking up on them. Resentments can form against family members and friends, or conversely the family and friends may grow resentful. Eventually, these resentments can build until they boil over; communication or actions turn volatile, and engagements could result with combative interchanges. If any trust and understanding had previously existed between the family and friends and the alcoholic/addict, this trust and understanding now may be dashed. Everyone may need to start over to build better relationships.

4. If they are comfortable in their recovery programs and starting to find satisfaction in understanding their addictions, they will bring them to the family and friends without prompting. It is important that the alcoholic/addict shares this as their special kind of pride. By asking, family and friends might take away their chance to boast and approach others with their new and exciting accomplishments.

5. Twelve Step meetings (or any other kind of recovery interactions) are personal. Newly recovering people may be embarrassed or ashamed to have to be "going through this." Monitoring might keep the shame alive.

6. The more others treat the recovery process as "standard operating procedure," the more that the alcoholic/addict will take recovery in stride and start to accept a new way of life.

7. If the alcoholic/addict invites others into their recovery, make sure that they lead the conversation. Family and friends should not become nosy or intrusive. They must keep in mind that in healthy dialogue, support people will be asking, not grilling. The words that family and friends use are crucial. Likewise, tone, inflection, and physical gestures can texture communication and be the difference between a positive or negative exchange. Don't

meet your loved one at the door, wringing your hands and hoping that all has gone well in the land of recovery. If you are anxious, your loved one will pick up on that and either be anxious as well or avoid you altogether.

A good, solid conversation about recovery could pave the way to other topics and start to establish or re-establish a trust and bond. Anytime your loved one terminates the conversation, let it be. It might have nothing to do with you, but take a moment to review your communication and do a mental checklist to make sure that you stayed neutral, didn't engage, and of course, didn't quiz or monitor. If you feel that you might have been a bit out of bounds, then find a calm, quiet time to apologize to the person. Be short and sweet! There is no need to defend or justify why you said something. It is enough to simply say, "Hey, I'm sorry for saying that. I can see that it's none of my business" or "I didn't mean to push my opinion on to you." If you get nothing but a grunt back, so be it. You are doing this to keep your side of the street clean while remaining honest and fair. Your motive here should be just that. It should have nothing to do your loved one's reaction or lack thereof.

Regardless of resentment, blame, or anger that your loved one may have directed at you, and though it may not seem like it, I believe the alcoholic/addict knows that you care, that you are worried, that you love them, and that you only want them to succeed and live a fruitful and productive life. The more that a person can accomplish on their own without others quizzing or monitoring, the better chance a person has to succeed.

If a man happens to find himself, he has a mansion which he can inhabit with dignity all the days of his life.
JAMES MICHENER

Chapter 12

ALLOW THE ALCOHOLIC / ADDICT TO REBUILD THEIR LIFE

One of the keys to a hopeful, strong and long-lasting recovery is allowing the alcoholic / addict to be responsible for their own actions and intentions. Whether the individual's concerns are about recovery, housing, employment, or social life, the more they come up with their own game plan, the more progress will be made in life generally and in addiction recovery specifically. The alcoholic / addict needs to rely on themselves for planning and developing this road map toward their goals.

They might ask for help, but try not to approach your loved one first or give them too much advice or direction. I have worked with too many parents who want to "fix" their children's self-esteem issues by strongly recommending that their children read certain books or attend motivational seminars. These well meaning parents think their children have suffered enough, and they want to promote the rebuilding of their children's lives. As a result, parents sometimes push their children's recoveries faster than is healthy or faster than the speed at which they are meant to unfold.

In letting the alcoholic / addict rebuild their life, you are giving them the opportunity to take on responsibility. In turn, they can't blame anyone else or use others as an excuse to relapse.

Don't be a crutch for another. Be mindful that in your zest and quest for being front and center and more than available to help your loved one embrace a clean and sober lifestyle, you are robbing your loved one of the chance to do some of their own footwork.

Your loved one's desire to rebuild their life may start before the recovery process is even underway. For example, if your loved one has approached you about seeking treatment, please don't trip over yourself getting to the computer to scan every residential or outpatient rehabilitation site. Allowing your loved one to first do some research will do two things. First, it reinforces their intention to be serious about the desire to get well. Second, it demonstrates that you are not running interference as you might have in the past.

Additionally, if your loved one approaches you with a desire to enter a recovery program (whether it is the first time or the tenth), try saying, "Congratulations, you must feel good about that decision. I would love to hear your thoughts or discuss what places you've found. If you'd like to get together to go over some of your options, just let me know." Say this instead of, "Thank God, you're finally going to do something about your problem. Here is a list of rehabilitation centers I've found that we should consider."

The first dialogue removes you from the picture. You are still expressing your regard for the decision, but also acknowledging that it is *their* decision not yours. Furthermore, you are testing the authenticity of your loved one's intentions by engaging them in doing work to find help for the problem. This serves as a good litmus test to prove how serious the alcoholic/addict is about changing this destructive lifestyle. Finally, by putting the onus on your loved one to search for a method of recovery that they will feel comfortable with, they can't blame you if it doesn't work out.

Allowing the alcoholic/addict to rebuild their life is an ongoing process. Even after years of practicing a clean and sober lifestyle, the alcoholic/addict needs to connect and reconnect with the world at their own pace, in many different areas. Like a scuba diver coming up from the depths of the ocean too quickly and experiencing the bends, if pushed too hard, too fast, or given a set of unrealistic expectations by well intending family members or friends, your loved one may suffer a relapse or extreme emotional distress.

I worked with Mark for many years to help him understand his son's addiction to methamphetamine. He was a kind, well-meaning parent, like all of my clients. As soon as his son showed a scintilla of leading a clean and sober lifestyle, Mark began to pepper him daily about what was on his agenda. If his son went on an interview and did not get the job, Mark would want to call the company and mount a campaign as to why they should hire his son and "give him a chance." Mark got an "A+" for the boundless efforts a parent will exact to help their child, but an "F" for not allowing his son to start rebuilding his own life his way.

Whether the alcoholic / addict is in a residential program, outpatient recovery program, a Twelve Step fellowship, or is quitting "cold turkey," this person needs to start earning credibility. Six months of accountability and responsible behavior is a good, healthy start to demonstrate the solid rebuilding of a clean and sober life.

In chapter 2, I discussed the acronym C.A.R.D. for what the friends and families of the alcoholic / addict *should expect* as the recovery process strengthens (this is different than expectations previously discussed). It is worth reviewing since it pertains to the rebuilding process.

Credibility
Accountability
Responsibility
Dependability

Again, be patient. Recovery is a long, hard road. There can be set-backs as well as victories. When the alcoholic / addict is ready to rebuild a new life through applied efforts it is truly a beautiful thing to behold. Please grant the alcoholic / addict the respect they have earned while they rebuild their physical, emotional, and psychological well being.

Each man's life represents a road toward himself.
HERMANN HESSE

Section Three

YOU ARE
AT THE HELM

This section is about you, on a more personal, independent level. It has nothing to do with your interaction with your loved one, but it's just about replenishing yourself and continuing to expand your horizons of self-awareness and substance abuse education.

Chapter 13

TAKING CARE OF YOU!

If you can't take care of yourself, you can't be of help to anyone else. Living with or loving an alcoholic / addict (whether in recovery or not) is an emotional, physical, and oftentimes, financial drain. It can leave you exhausted before you even get out of bed in the morning. In this chapter, I offer concepts that I have implemented in my daily life and introduced to my clients.

Replenish yourself. Whether you get weekly massages, practice yoga, swim, hop into your Jacuzzi, hike, or spend five minutes quietly praying each morning and night, it is important to shut off your brain, take deep breaths, and focus on your own center core. Replenishment time is a quiet time between you and whatever you spiritually connect with.

When I was going through a particularly difficult time in my life, distressed over my loved one's addiction issues, questioning career choices, and marital ones, I found a mantra that I would repeat as many as fifty times a day, "I'm working toward better days ahead." It was simple, but hearing it out loud gave me hope and encouragement and was my way of replenishing myself—shutting my brain off to too much jibberish. It was nonjudgmental, no pressure, and I didn't set any specific goals for myself. If the day found me only brushing my teeth and walking the dog, so be it; other days might find me repainting my bedroom. Either way, I was working toward better days ahead—at my speed, through my way. These seven words kept me focused and confident that if I put one foot in front of the other (no matter how small the step), kept a positive attitude, and stayed open minded to what might present itself, I knew one day I would reach those "better days" that I had hoped and prayed for. In chapter 15, I will discuss the importance of slogans, mantras, and other mental comforts, as they can enhance one's world of personal replenishment.

Do volunteer work. Nothing is better for the soul than getting away from focusing on oneself. Taking time once or twice a week to do volunteer work is not only rewarding, but it also allows you to step back, to give of yourself, and to feel grateful for all that you have. When so much of your life has revolved around the alcoholic / addict, it can be a peaceful breath of fresh air to do simple things for others without fear of judgment or reprimand, but heartfelt appreciation.

I love horses and dogs, so I volunteer at a therapeutic riding academy and stroll with my Golden Retriever, Lucy, at the local hospital. Once a week, Lucy wags her tail and spreads slobbery cheer to all the cancer patients. It is something I am dedicated to, and it is on my calendar regardless of how I am feeling that day. I realize that it is likely that no one would miss me or my dog if we didn't show up, but it's important to be accountable to the commitments I have made to others, and it helps me to stay humble and grateful.

Suit up and show up. If you have a job (outside of the home or not, income producing or not), then taking care of your responsibilities is vital to reclaiming your own personal sense of purpose. Whether it provides a real paycheck or an emotional paycheck, work confirms that you are doing something that's important to you and possibly to your family, and it's validation for services rendered.

My client Heidi has her own business with her husband. Her daughter calls her approximately fifteen times a day (no exaggeration). I have advised Heidi to express to her daughter that when she is at work, any more than two calls a day is unacceptable unless there is a genuine emergency. Taking care of yourself in your place of business, regardless of what you do or how you spend your time doing it, is important for retaining your respect and dignity.

Find your passion. I have previously discussed the importance of the alcoholic / addict finding a passion to take the place of their former drinking or drug buddy. Refocusing one's time, energy, emotions, and physical state is one of the key factors toward developing a successful and satisfying clean and sober lifestyle.

The same is true for the family member or friend who has spent so much time thinking and focusing on their loved one. Chances are you have probably ignored the fun and exciting things in your life. Recapture those! Reinstate an old passion or find a new one that you can sink your teeth into and look forward to participating in. Whether it's bird watching, painting, bowling, book club, or learning how to play bridge, jump in with both feet.

When I was consumed with my daughter's addiction, I desperately needed a distraction. I poured my energy into taking tennis lessons. In doing so, I began to enjoy other aspects of my life, and I met new and interesting friends while staying fit and healthy. For years, this book had become my passion. I was going through some very trying personal times and was grateful that I could lose myself in the private complexities of writing.

While finding your passion, make sure that you have a "B" plan or "alternative airport," as I sometimes like to say. A "B" plan is important and also has a calming effect on you if your "A" plan does not come to fruition; it should be as well thought out as the "A" plan.

For example: you give yourself one year to see your passion take root (starting a catering company, writing a book, going back to school to learn a trade or profession). If you don't feel like you have made some significant headway by the time that scheduled date rolls around, then move on to plan "B" (taking a nonentrepreneurial job, writing short stories instead of your novel, taking a different class, or exiting the scholastic world altogether).

When we can see our path and get excited about it (whether it includes the alcoholic / addict or not), we can start to relax and focus on our plans and the commitment at hand. We also know there is an alternative if it doesn't work out.

One more thought: avoid vagueness as much as possible. It's very easy to say, "I'll see what happens with this" or "I don't need to pin anything down right now." Keep on track and on schedule. Having dates to strive toward is more responsible and calming in the long run than just bumping along the bottom and going with whatever may come.

Do your own research on addiction. Investigate the substance that you believe your loved one is using or may be addicted to. Opinions and facts are different. Stick to the facts and not the opinions of well-meaning friends who could cloud your head with misinformation. Knowledge is power. The more you know about your loved one's addiction, and its characteristics and traits, the more confident you can be in a conversation regarding their specific situation. You won't be caught off guard or caught up on another's opinion if you've already done your own research. That said, don't overload yourself by spending countless hours reading about what amounts to quite depressing material. The description of heroin and its side effects will not change no matter how many sources you check out.

Be wary of well-meaning advice. Please don't take the advice of family members and friends as gospel. Although they are only trying to be of help, listen politely, and then formulate your own conclusion. They may strongly suggest that you do one thing or another. However, even if they have experienced a similar situation, remember that everyone's issues are different, and complex dynamics come into play. What might have worked for them may not work for you.

My client Marcy was having lunch with friends. She confided in them about her concerns regarding her addicted son. Each one of her friends had reported similar concerns with their loved ones and strongly advised her to go home and immediately drug test him. Marcy had never drug tested her son nor had they ever had that understanding between them. However, Marcy went home armed with a pharmaceutical drug kit and demanded her son urinate in the cup. The test came up positive, but now what?

Since there had been no rules or regulations established between the two of them regarding the use of illicit drugs in the home, both ended up resentful and confused about what the next step would or should be. Though Marcy's intentions could be construed as the actions of a parent very concerned about her loved one, she acted out of impulse, as her friends fanned the flames for her to take action.

Marcy should have sought out professional advice regarding the steps she needed to take to deal in a healthy and productive manner with her son and his addiction, and not advice over a Caesar salad with friends.

Be mindful to whom you talk. You might want to think twice about discussing your struggles or a loved one's addiction issues with friends, certain family members, or relatives. This is not because you are ashamed or fearful of their judgment, but because you may be opening yourself up to their advice or opinion. It could put an unnecessary strain on your relationships, especially if you don't take the advice. Also, friendships can be very precarious and delicate. Although your friend might ache for your pain and suffering, if that's all you end up talking about it may become too much of a burden for the person to handle. Additionally, information regarding your loved one's addiction could prove detrimental if it finds its way to the workplace or is brought into other relationships. Remember, no matter how upset you are, or how desperate you feel to unload your burden, be respectful of your loved one's privacy. Unless they give you permission to discuss their situation openly or with certain individuals, allow them to tell who they want, when they want.

Don't change your basic core. The alcoholic / addict is not going to stay clean and sober because you've switched from being a Republican to a Democrat, nor will they relapse because you've decided to cut your hair. Don't give your loved one that kind of subconscious "power." You are who you are. You were that person before addiction became part of your mutual landscape, and you will remain that same person if or when your loved one adopts a clean and sober lifestyle.

However, be open minded to issues that your loved one may have difficulty dealing with or accepting, which is something you can easily change without much effort or without compromising yourself. These issues or confrontations might have helped perpetuate the addiction. It is the healthy individual who can look at their own side of the street and take responsibility for actions or lack of actions. Relationships are built on give and take, listening and talking. If your loved one shares that certain things or people in your life make him or her uncomfortable, do your best to respect and appreciate where the person is coming from, and consider modifying the situation. Make sure that these suggestions are coming from a place of genuine concern and are not laying the groundwork for an easy argument or threatening a relapse if you don't acquiesce.

Don't change your schedule or routine. Too often, friends or family members become anxious about leaving their loved one alone for fear of their use of drugs or alcohol. If your loved one does relapse, then they were already going to and there is nothing you can do about it.

I counseled the Strauss family, who were not going to pay for their son's apartment. They felt that while he lived under their roof they could monitor his drug addiction and could keep him from getting into trouble.

He needed to make his own mistakes to decide what way of life he wanted to pursue. Instead, he became very complacent living at home, doing whatever he wanted, whenever he wanted. There were no consequences as long as he stayed within their sight. Ironically, instead of accepting his easy, nonresponsible lifestyle, he may grow more resentful toward his parents, and maybe even himself, as he realizes that he has allowed them to dictate his future.

Watch your boundaries. I have repeated this theory many times throughout this book, but its importance justifies reiteration. Remember that no matter how hard you try, or how important it may be to you, if the alcoholic / addict does not want to alter their lifestyle, then there is nothing you can do or say that will change their mind.

Allow your loved one to ask you for help. Don't take the beginning of this important journey away from them by stepping in with your idea or opinion of recovery options. As hard as it is, let your loved one come to you. It will mean more to both of you in the long run, and it is the only way that a true and honest recovery can take root.

If you are a natural rescuer, the concept of implementing boundaries might be exceptionally difficult, as your loved one with an addiction is the perfect person for you to "rescue" and validate your own worth. Don't make this your purpose in life, as the alcoholic / addict might exploit it emotionally, psychologically, and financially, and you deserve better.

Know your options. I have often told my clients that they have options regarding their life with the alcoholic / addict. Remember, this book is not about how you can change your loved one and the addiction, but about needing to take care of yourself regardless of how your loved one will respond.

When my clients Mark and Allison came to me for counseling, Mark admitted that he felt he had a drinking problem and wanted to cut down, but he was not entirely ready to stop. I relayed to Mark that it was his decision alone whether he wanted to stop drinking, but that he needed to be aware of the consequences of his drinking with regard to Allison's actions.

Here are three basic options that I see a family member or friend having if their loved one wants to drink or use drugs. These would be discussed with your loved one as being your right to react the way you want, as it pertains to the consequences of their addictive behavior:

1. **Do nothing.** Accept the person in their addiction. Getting angry or fighting the next day about it is a waste of time. You have decided that the effort to change things for yourself is just not in the cards right now. Okay, no judgment, but keep to that decision. It is not fair to you or the alcoholic/addict if one minute you do nothing about their alcoholic intake or drug abuse and the next you throw them out of the house for the same infraction. If in time you want to change your posture, do so in a planned out, nonvolatile way.

2. **Do something.** Discuss a plan that will be put into effect if the person chooses to participate in their addiction. Perhaps the plan involves them not coming home that night, or if they do, the doors will be locked, the lights turned out, and entrance will not be an option. If you are strong enough to implement a call to the police when their state of inebriation is unacceptable, make sure they know this and that you are ready, willing, and able to follow through with the plan. Another solution might be a plan to spend a night (or two) out of the house. If this does not prove satisfying, you may feel more time is needed like a week or even a month.

3. **Do the extreme.** You may decide that you cannot live with your loved one who does not want to learn to live a clean and sober lifestyle. You may feel that there is no option left for you but to make a drastic change and move out for an extended period of time. During this time, both you and the alcoholic/addict can decide your course of action, either separately or together.

Mark was very uncomfortable knowing the possibility existed that his wife moving out altogether could be an option. I explained that it wasn't equitable for him to do as he pleased, while she could not do what was best for herself.

The following five suggestions are more about being present. They don't require an emotional plan, just a time commitment, and, good news, they don't involve any interaction with the alcoholic/addict. I have personally found these suggestions very helpful while I was struggling with my loved ones' addiction issues.

1. **Attend open Alcoholics Anonymous meetings** (meetings open to anyone with or without an addiction issue)

Here you can be inconspicuous and won't be called upon to say anything, yet you are afforded the opportunity to listen to alcoholic/addicts. This can be a profound and eye-opening experience, as these meetings are usually "speaker meetings" where one individual talks for the bulk of the meeting and traces their life from dysfunction and destruction to recovery. You can hear firsthand the same plight that your loved one may be experiencing from someone else, affording you some distance and objectivity. Understanding that someone else has been able to embrace sobriety may give you hope as well. If your loved one welcomes a Twelve Step recovery program, then they may appreciate that you are getting involved in your own way. Regardless of whether they approve or not, remember that you are doing this for your own education. There is a lot to be learned from these meetings, and it is the first place I would start to gather honest and genuine information about the disease.

2. **Attend Al-Anon meetings** (meetings for the friends and families of the alcoholic/addict)

I have been attending Al-Anon meetings for twenty years. The camaraderie and spirituality that knits this special group of family and friends together is worth much more than the dollar contribution. Al-Anon is not for everyone, but give it a good chance. Start easy and slow; attend beginner's meetings and ones with no particular format (unlike a book or step study meeting). Listen to what the other members have to say; often they attribute their health and happiness to what they have learned by attending these meetings. Attending these meetings helps them to learn how to accept the alcoholic/addict in their life. You will hear at each meeting that "You didn't cause it, you can't control it, and you can't cure it." Thoughtful and wise words to help the family member or friend begin to accept the powerlessness they have over their loved one's addiction. Also, some of the shares are truly priceless, and you will think about them over and over again. One of my favorites was when a woman shared that she would like to be the alcoholic, as she was actually jealous of the constant attention they were getting day in and day out.

Al-Anon presents a very strong "higher power" viewpoint, as they believe no one can regain control of an out-of-control life if they don't surrender their will and care to something larger than themselves. Please don't be turned off by this. It can be a very warm and comforting feeling knowing that you don't have to be alone as you walk this dark road of addiction. You can participate regardless of your personal beliefs and gain a great deal.

I believe the alcoholic/addict would benefit from attending Al-Anon meetings as well. Learning about how the family members and friends deal with addiction issues in their own Twelve Step recovery programs will shed more light and only add more fulfillment and satisfaction to the person with the addiction. Al-Anon also provides some wonderful books to read. *Courage to Change* and *One Day at a Time* are two books that have daily passages of concepts and spirituality important to the program. I read a passage daily, as it usually points out something for me to think about or reflect upon.

3. Attend Coda, Alateen, ACA meetings

Attend those meetings specifically geared toward your special recovery needs. Coda meetings can shed some helpful insight for the codependent, enabler, or rescuer. Alateen meetings are for the teenager with a family member or friend who is struggling with addiction issues. ACA (Adult Children of Alcoholics) meetings are designed for adult children who grew up with alcoholic parents or guardians.

Self-help groups are excellent. They provide a safe and confidential place for men and women to go and share their experience, strength, and hope. Even if you never open your mouth, it can be very comforting to know that you are not alone. Chances are you will gain some valuable and important insight into how others deal with their loved one's substance abuse issues.

4. Seek professional counseling

If your world takes on a different dynamic because your loved one continues to remain in addiction or because they are working toward a clean and sober lifestyle, issues will arise during your own recovery process. You might consider obtaining the help of a professional addiction counselor, not just a marriage and family therapist. It would be beneficial to seek a counselor who has had a personal journey in this field and can relate from firsthand experience as well as professional training.

Whether you are rebuilding your relationship with your friend, child, mate, or sibling, these are very tender times for both of you. This process should be handled with respect, dignity, a gentle, but strong guiding hand, and above all no judgment.

5. Watch movies that help educate

Though difficult to watch, there are some insightful and informative movies that portray addiction as their central theme. Here are a few I recommend:

- *My Name is Bill W*—A television movie starring James Woods and James Garner. The story traces the lives of Bill Wilson and Dr. Bob, the founders of Alcoholics Anonymous.
- *When Love is Not Enough: The Lois Wilson Story*—A television movie starring Winona Ryder and Barry Pepper as Lois and Bill Wilson. This movie focuses on the life of the co-founder of the Al-Anon Family Groups Twelve Step recovery program; a program born out of necessity for understanding and living with an alcoholic.
- *The Days of Wine and Roses*—One of the first movies to portray the devastation of alcohol dependency in a family. Lee Remick and Jack Lemmon struggle together and then independently with their addictions.
- *The Man with the Golden Arm*—A powerful black and white movie with Frank Sinatra as a heroin addict trying desperately to stay clean.
- *Gaslight*—Another classic, starring Charles Boyer and Ingrid Bergman. Though addiction is not a theme in this movie, Charles Boyer plots to drive Ingrid Bergman crazy by telling her one thing and implementing another. Impossible to follow the bouncing ball of what is expected

of her, she questions her own sanity. I liken this to the mental gymnastics someone can put their family members or friends through due to their addiction and duplicitous behavior.

- *Clean and Sober*—Starring Michael Keaton as a man avoiding rehabilitation for a cocaine habit, and who eventually succumbs to an honest recovery.
- *When a Man Loves a Woman*—Meg Ryan plays an alcohol addicted wife and mother desperate to regain control of her life and family, as her husband (played by Andy Garcia) is trying to understand the ramifications of the disease.
- *28 Days*—Sandra Bullock is outstanding as a young woman with an alcoholic addiction. She attends a twenty-eight day residential recovery program after ruining her sister's wedding due to her out of control and inebriated behavior.
- *The Basketball Diaries*—Based on a true story, a young Leonardo DiCaprio portrays a fun-loving youth who gets entangled with the underground world of heroin. One of the most gut-wrenching and honest scenes I have witnessed in any movie is between DiCaprio's character and his mother when she is torn between giving him money (knowing it would be going to his addiction) and calling the police. With money in one hand and the phone receiver in another, she sobs on the floor as she deals with the despair of her impending decision. A must see for anyone whose child is dealing with addiction issues and the deep love, fear, and frustration that any parent endures.
- *City by the Sea*—Robert De Niro plays a detective caught between his duty to arrest his falsely accused, drug-addicted son for murder and his parental love and enabling.
- *Rachel Getting Married*—Academy award nominee Anne Hathaway portrays a young woman in a rehabilitation program who is returning home to face a challenging weekend in celebration of her sister's wedding.
- *Crazy Heart*—Academy award-winning actor Jeff Bridges portrays a middle aged, alcohol addicted country/western singer. Losing a very important relationship due to irresponsible behavior because of his alcohol dependency,

Bridges commits to rehab and a clean and sober lifestyle, which slowly starts to turn his life around toward the positive.

Phew, there's a lot to think about when learning to take care of yourself. Be patient. It doesn't have to happen in one week or one month, nor should it, as burn out is not something we are striving for. Do what you can when you can, but do something each and every day. Even if it's just reading a passage from a spiritual book or taking a long bubble bath, the osmosis of being kinder and gentler with yourself will start to pay off with newfound strength and resolve.

Be not afraid of growing slowly;
be afraid only of standing still.
CHINESE PROVERB

Chapter 14

EXERCISES FOR YOUR
OWN PERSONAL GROWTH

This chapter is designed to teach you some personal activities that I share with my clients as well as ones I practice myself. They are very simple, and chances are you may already be incorporating some of them into your daily, weekly, or monthly routines.

Recite "The Serenity Prayer"

Before I close my eyes at night, I silently say "The Serenity Prayer." It is the creed to Twelve Step recovery programs and the keystone to Alcoholics Anonymous and Al-Anon alike. Whether you are an ardent member of a self-help program or they just aren't for you, "The Serenity Prayer" is universal, and its words encompass everything and all things.

If you are not familiar with "The Serenity Prayer," it goes like this:

> God, grant me the serenity
> to accept the things I cannot change,
> the courage to change the things I can,
> and the wisdom to know the difference.

Every word, every sentence is powerful and presents a challenge to the most grounded and confident of individuals whether in substance abuse recovery or not. The words *serenity, acceptance, change, courage,* and *wisdom* are intensely thought provoking, individually as well as knitted together.

Take some time to think about the words and how they relate to you personally as well as your interaction with your loved one—the alcoholic / addict. This creed provides great comfort and assurance to me as I deal with my own conflicts with or without the presence of the alcoholic / addict in my life.

Practice Journaling

Journaling is great. I don't mean the "Dear Diary" type that we all practiced in junior high, but writing down concepts, thoughts, phrases, issues, or anything that comes up during the day that you find thought provoking and can reflect on later. Write about the pleasant as well as the uncomfortable. You might see things differently the next day, month, or even year.

I think it's great to journal a few sentences or paragraphs in the morning. Maybe jot down what you hope to accomplish that day, whether with confidence or trepidation. At the end of the day, reread your morning entry, and make a written comment as to how the day fared, what you were pleased with, and what might still need some work.

This is your own personal framework, your private path. No one else need be privy to it unless you wish to share it. Your journaling may have nothing to do with the alcoholic / addict and it's perfectly okay if it just pertains to you and your needs. Identifying your own personal triggers and issues can be very helpful if you write them down when they are fresh in your mind. You might be able to see a pattern that has everything or nothing to do with your loved one's addiction, and where you are in your life today.

Write a Gratitude List

A kissing cousin to journaling is the gratitude list. Dealing with drugs and alcohol in your life is draining and exhausting. A lot of negative energy can eventually weigh down even the most positive person. Hence, the gratitude list is vital. Once a day or once a week, either on paper or aloud, list who and what you are grateful for.

Try not to sit on the pity-pot and say that life sucks and you have nothing to be grateful for. I know it sometimes can be very difficult to find anything positive in your life especially if your loved one is nowhere to be found, in jail, or deep in addiction. Nevertheless, negative energy breeds a negative outlook, and it's just as easy to find something to be grateful for as it is to wring your hands in despair and fear.

You can list things as simple as being alive to see a beautiful sunset, the unconditional love of a pet, your favorite food for dinner, or witnessing your own growth and confidence in all variety of areas in your life.

Don't be shy. Spread your wings and be unbridled about your gratitude. It will make you smile and realize that there are many special things in your life that make your life worth living—things that are unique to you alone.

The Fireside Chat with Friends in Common

I have found success in organizing a bimonthly small group gathering of five or six individuals. Coming together to discuss communication and boundaries surrounding themselves and their loved ones is an excellent way to share ideas and thoughts. I have implemented these sessions in my home, and I make them safe, comfortable, and confidential. These "fireside chats" allow family and friends to share their trials and tribulations as well as the fears and anxieties that they are going through with the alcoholic/addict. Unlike Al-Anon, where cross talk is not permitted during the meeting, I encourage everyone to ask questions or share from their own experiences.

To do this yourself, find a handful of friends who are experiencing the same life challenges you are and meet for coffee or lunch somewhere safe. No one in the group should pontificate with expert advice or stand in judgment of others. Instead, everyone should strive to provide strength, hope, and an honest exchange of communication. If possible, elicit the guidance of a professional addiction counselor. A counselor's presence will help to keep the discussion focused, and you will have someone who can jump in as a mediator if need be.

Play "As Fate Would Have It"

This is a simple exercise I have enjoyed noodling around in my brain when I'm bored or have time on my hands. Mentally, I plot all the major incidents of my life when I thought I was on a concrete path toward my goals, yet something transpired that would lead me away from that life. For example, I had a successful career, loved playing tennis, and truly believed that I would be doing both for the rest of my life. However, unexpected twists and turns started to lead me down a different road. At the time, I was fearful of the outcome and wondered what had happened to change the comfortable path I had established.

As I look back, these situations were a blessing in disguise or "as fate would have it," as I had no option but to allow myself to embrace and trust the journey. Today, my career is the opposite of what I had been doing for twenty years. And tennis? Well, I got burned out and replaced my racket with yoga.

Relive the small occurrences that changed your path or presented something different to what you were thinking. We all have said something similar to, "I really didn't want to go to that party, but if I hadn't, I wouldn't have met my spouse or found a new career." Certain people and situations that come into our lives unexpectedly can have a major hand in rearranging our journey for the better and propelling us toward goals and dreams that we thought were not possible. In the recovery community this is what is called "a God shot" or an "Ah-Ha" moment. The more you can recall these incidents, the more you will find comfort that you will be taken care of—maybe not how you think you want it to be, or not in your time frame, but believe me, it will come together one way or another. Of course you will find yourself saying, "Why did I worry so much and waste so much time or energy on this, when it has ultimately worked out perfectly."

Build a House of Personal Fulfillment

This exercise is like a kaleidoscope. It can change with a turn of the wrist—momentarily, daily, monthly, or yearly. Sometimes, we spend so much time worrying about our loved one, we forget about what's important in our own lives. This exercise breaks down what I believe to be areas in our lives that make us personally feel good, feel content, feel fulfilled; it has nothing to do with the alcoholic/addict.

In this exercise, you have a "house" with seven rooms. The number of filled rooms can indicate how content you are. It is best to have at least four of your seven rooms filled to feel safe and satisfying. These rooms bring you joy and contentment and can establish your purpose in life and what's important. These rooms make you who you are, individually and separately from the pack.

I have listed seven primary rooms for fulfillment. I think it covers the basics for most people. Please feel free to add your own personal rooms or delete ones that have no purpose for you. If the majority of the rooms in your life are not fulfilling, satisfying, and inviting, examine why and see how you can change that. It might take time, effort, and a new perspective. Reflect upon your life, and if you feel that you are coming up short, think about redirecting some of your priorities.

Once you've assembled your list of rooms, put it away. Take it out again in six months or a year and see what (if anything) has changed. If you can identify what is missing, or what has strengthened, you can better maximize your efforts to stay on course or perpetuate some change. All people's lists will be different according to what "rooms" are most important to them. The first room listed is the most important and the others are built on its foundation.

1. **Health.** Without health, it is hard for you to enjoy or find contentment, happiness, or fulfillment in your life. I sometimes take my health for granted, but when I have to deal with the flu or a surgical procedure, my mind is wrapped around the fragility and vulnerability of my body and human life.

2. **Companionship.** While some people prefer to be alone, others may feel that they are not complete without the friendship and love of a mate or companion. Sharing your ups and downs with someone whom you trust unconditionally is what makes you whole. The intimacy that two people share is their armor in a united front that can make them feel invincible to the world. However, if the relationship is not steeped in respect and commonality, your own companionship can be very fulfilling. Don't compromise your needs just to be in a relationship. Don't be afraid to be alone. You may be surprised how full this room can be with just a party of one.

3. **Children/Family.** Many people have no mate or companion, but they share a tight bond with their children, family of origin, or extended family. Surely parents love their children unconditionally, and from the day of a child's birth a connection is established

that will never be broken. Close families are there for each other both in times of celebration and in times of need. It doesn't matter if the physical proximity of the family members is two streets away or several area codes, this relationship can be one of unwavering kinship and friendship.

4. **Money/Job.** Some people live to work. Their job is what defines them. The motivation for their work can range from financial prosperity to feeding their ego or fulfilling themselves through quiet philanthropic or volunteer work. Unless you don't need to, most people spend the bulk of their lives working. Satisfaction in the workplace can often set the stage for one's happiness in other areas. If you hate going to work, that negativity will bleed into other aspects of your life. Having money can definitely make one's life easier in certain ways, but it will never complete you.

5. **Friends/Pets.** Are the two interchangeable? To many, yes. Some people find their pets to be their best friends and wouldn't have it any other way. The unconditional love, the tail wagging or purring that is there day in and day out when you walk through the door, or in my case, the nickering of my horse when I approach him with a carrot is immensely fulfilling. People love their pets as part of the family. And why not? Who else could look so cute hanging out the window of the car with their ears flapping in the wind? On the other hand, some people find that their circle of human friends is what they need to keep them happy and content. What would Carrie Bradshaw from *Sex and the City* do without her friends? They talk to each other ten times a day and have at least two meals a day together. However, good friends are hard to come by. Most people say that they can count their good friends on one hand and wouldn't trade that companionship and loyalty for anything in the world.

6. **Hobbies/Sports.** Ask professional athletes what the most important thing in their lives are and they will likely answer sports. Just as some people identify with their job, for athletes, their sport is what and who they are. Most of us aren't professional athletes, but

we can watch the sport networks 24/7 and bemoan the one month a year when there are virtually no sports of interest being televised. People's sports can be very important to them; they consider their teams to be kindred spirits. Some people won't plan a vacation if the play-offs are on, or will zigzag across the country to watch their alma mater play ball. Years ago in my home, it was a hallowed day when the basketball brackets were announced for "March Madness." Hobbies, goals, and passions can be just as infectious—from collecting stamps to rebuilding Harleys, whether a solo endeavor or a joint effort, they are very rewarding. They offer a strong sense of personal accomplishment and hold a special place in the heart of their practitioners. If one finds the right hobby or passion it can be a lifesaver for when you are feeling "less than" or under the weather emotionally or psychologically.

7. **Religion/Spirituality.** For people who devote their life to God, Buddha, Jesus, or their own religious calling, spirituality can encompass their being. Their contentment and satisfaction is reaped by a belief in a deity that they feel is justified and right. Some find that religion is part of their daily routine. Spirituality can include the formality of religion or may just be the consciousness of life's daily blessings. People who do not subscribe to an organized religion may find inner contentment, calm, and peace in embracing an omnipresent power that can be found anywhere, anytime. Spirituality can make us feel that we are not alone. Whatever your specific beliefs, spirituality can be alive in all of us. It is a wonderful silent partner, a copilot that courses through our being seven days a week, twenty-four hours a day. You can call upon it whenever it feels necessary. One last thought: call upon and trust your spirituality or religion, for it is often what is needed to help quell a busy, unsettled mind from churning in the murky waters of addiction.

Break Down Your Resentments

In order to have a complete and honest recovery, you need to examine some insecurities and uncomfortable attributes. Anger and resentment that remain bottled up inside can fester, and if not dealt with, they can explode into other areas of your life. You may take it out on other people who have nothing to do with the resentment you are harboring.

Everyone experiences resentment; it is part of life. Use the breakdown that follows to cope with resentment that may or may not be directly related to the alcoholic / addict in your life.

Giving proper and due credit to the Twelve Steps of Alcoholics Anonymous, A.A. has incorporated a step that deals with the person's resentment toward others. Step four is an important part of recovery where the person addicted to alcohol closely examines resentment, which may continue to be alive and well for years after sobriety. Most likely, resentment has contributed greatly to one's life of addiction.

Without cleaning out the skeletons of resentment, neither a person with addiction issues nor a friend or family member can resolve the baggage that hampers recovery. In Alcoholics Anonymous, the person addicted to alcohol usually works with a sponsor to reconstruct their resentments—past and present. This is called an inventory and takes place through a series of questions and answers that the person in addiction recovery works on privately in their own time frame. Upon completion, the alcoholic goes over this work with a personal sponsor, and together they dissect how resentments have created havoc in the person's life.

If you are currently involved in an Al-Anon program, you may already be doing this step with your sponsor. If you do not have a "sponsor" (someone who helps guide you through the Al-Anon program regarding challenges you may be facing about recovery) from a Twelve Step program to go over this with, work with a professional counselor. You might want to think twice about sharing this list of resentments with family members since they may not understand your feelings or may appear on the list and take offense.

Even if you were not dealing with addiction, this resentment grid would be a good way of working on and keeping a healthy state of mind. There isn't a person in the world who doesn't have resentments and could not benefit from this exercise.

Remember that this does not have to be done in a single day. Take your time. Do a little each day or when you are in a particularly positive place so as not to beat yourself up with guilt, remorse, or producing fresh resentments. I believe that the better we are feeling about ourselves the more honest we can be because we are grounded in positive energy.

For those to whom this is a new concept, answer the four questions honestly, slowly, and over time. This is not a race. It takes thought and courage to benefit from this exercise.

"Whom or what am I resentful toward"?

The answer can range from a person to an institution (a bank, the police department). You can be fifty years old and be resentful that you didn't pursue a better collegiate opportunity when you had the chance. You can be resentful that you were never picked first or second to field a softball team. No resentment is too small to note if it is still taking up space somewhere in your head.

Don't feel guilty if the first person you name is the alcoholic / addict in your life. It is only normal that you resent that person for not only messing up their own life but for creating chaos in many other lives. You can be resentful about someone's behavior or about the personality changes due to addiction and still love that person.

When you start putting these resentments down on paper, don't be surprised if you find yourself just as frustrated or angry as you were when those situations first happened. This is unfinished business. This unfinished business might not be the center of your daily focus, but you cannot move on to work on current issues if you haven't cleaned the closet of the old ones.

In the years I spent dealing with my own loved one's addiction and recovery, I made several fourth-step resentment grids. Over time, I added new resentments and deleted others as my life has taken on different scenarios. I have kept them all and used them as references to compare and contrast where I was then to where I am today.

"What are the resentments I have?"

These dictate more specific answers and can be numerous. Start with the big, obvious ones like, "I'm resentful that my husband is an alcoholic, and I can't trust his actions when he drinks too much." Or you might write, "I'm resentful that my daughter doesn't care about school anymore and is becoming irresponsible."

Work your way toward the medium ones like, "I'm resentful that my boss did not promote me." Or write, "I'm resentful about the weight reduction program I'm on because they told me I would lose weight faster."

The small ones can read like, "I'm resentful that my favorite restaurant is going out of business." Or you might write, "I'm resentful that there are no more *Seinfeld* reruns on TV."

Parents (whether alive or not) and other members of your family unit will most likely rank high in unfinished business or resentments. Rarely do people share that they had an idyllic childhood or upbringing. Usually there are one or more adults closely connected to the family who may have done or said something along the way and thereby planted the seed of resentment.

Don't forget the past. Your past experiences are really important because, while you don't want to dwell on old issues, you don't want to close the door on the lessons either. Past resentments can hamper healthy growth and development, not only yours, but anyone's. Divorce, being uprooted, illness, unintentional physical injury, mental abuse, or physical abuse can lead to resentments that may plague you for years, no matter how diligent you are in dealing with them emotionally and psychologically. Even relatively small resentments from the past, like not being asked to your senior prom, can contribute to building blocks of poor self-esteem, questionable self-worth, and ultimately, resentment.

It's important to note that just because you face your resentments with an open and honest attitude does not mean that they will magically disappear. Resentments never really go away, but the objective here is to address them and accept them for the part they played in your life. We can't change anything now, so why spend time going over the "shoulda, woulda, coulda?"

Knowledge and acceptance (and acceptance doesn't mean being weak or giving in) help you to step back and look at the big picture of our life. Acceptance enables you to view your past as your own personal road map to learn more about what you might or might not want to change.

"These resentments affect me how?"

Resentments make us angry, fearful, insecure, uncomfortable, unloved, distrusting, paranoid, and intimidated, to name just a few emotions. Do these steps for each resentment that you have identified:

1. Write down how each of your different resentments affected you then and how they affect you now.
2. Continue by discussing how you dealt with the emotion caused in you then and how you are dealing with it now (and why).

"What is my part?"

This is the most difficult part of the exercise. In order for the whole process to be effective, it requires total honesty and real soul-searching.

Remember that nobody is going to read this unless you want them to, so you are an audience of one.

Ego is usually the biggest stumbling block to unfettered honesty. "I did nothing wrong, it was all her/his fault," is a common hue and cry. There are situations where one is presented with a no-fault scenario, such as with emotional or physical abuse. No child is responsible for the divorce of their parents, and nothing warrants physical or mental abuse.

Look at the part you played in a simple, almost ordinary situation where you feel resentment. It can go something like this, "I am resentful toward my parents for kicking me out of the house before I was ready to live on my own." What is my part? It could be, "I was irresponsible about keeping my word to them regarding curfew or household chores," "I was frequently in trouble with school or the law," and "I ignored the second and third warnings they gave me when I did not do as they asked."

Looking closely and carefully at your part of the resentment puts it on a more level playing field. Seeing your part helps those resentments take on a more human dimension, so you can see the picture more clearly and therefore accept sharing the blame.

This section was packed with a variety of exercises from the simplest to ones that require more time and thought. Some may be just what you need or having been looking for; others might not float your boat. However, over the years, my clients have enjoyed implementing some of these exercises, and together we have come up with new ones. They enjoy sharing them with me or some of their friends, for often there is new or different light shed, depending on where they are in their lives and what challenges they are dealing with at that time. Flex your mental and emotional muscles; it can be fun and productive and you might surprise yourself with revelations and discoveries you come up with that you didn't even know existed.

To improve the golden moment of opportunity,
and catch the good that is within our reach,
is the great art of life.
SAMUEL JOHNSON

Chapter 15

SLOGANS AND MANTRAS— THE MENTAL COMFORTS

We all have our favorite sayings or chants that over the years have become our own personal signatures. Sometimes they are only special to us and no one is privy to them; others are spouted out in daily conversation. Often, they are part of our upbringing, and if heard enough, can even shape who we are. My father was fond of saying, "Lead, follow, or get out of the way" and "You can do it just as well as the next person, maybe even better." In this chapter, the slogans and mantras that I am discussing are more of a mental comfort as opposed to expressive, visual quips aimed at anyone who is in earshot.

Al-Anon Twelve—Step Recovery Slogans

The Al-Anon Twelve Step recovery program has been an integral part of my life for many, many years. The most consistent comfort I have gotten out of the program is from their slogans. With gratitude and thanks to Al-Anon, I have listed them in no particular order and attached my own personal view of their meaning and how they affect me. Even if you don't attend Al-Anon, you may find some resolve and peace in having them swim through your mind as you are faced with the challenges of the alcoholic/addict in your life.

Think—that's what the brain is for

It denotes an ability to reason, dissect, and weigh the pros and cons of our decisions. Real thinking can take some practice and patience. Too often we react on the spur of the moment from something we don't like seeing or hearing. Hitting the pause button allows us to utilize our all powerful brain and analyze what was said and how we can process our next move in a healthy and confident manner.

How important is it?

I have found this to be one of the most important and frequent slogans that I call upon. When I am faced with a situation or confrontation that I am not comfortable with, I quietly say, "How important is it"? Usually when I take a moment to ask myself this, I realize that digging my heels in and allowing my ego to demand that I prove my point is just not that important. If a situation merits a discussion, then so be it, but if it's about pointing out that you were right about something or debating small, picky issues, then forget it and move on. I often view this slogan as if it were an electronic ticker tape going round and round in Times Square. It's a powerfully visual reminder for me, and one that checks my attitude and communication instantly.

Just for today

Deal with today and only today. Your decisions and actions are only for today; the past is the past and the future is unknown. Planning is productive and should be implemented more for tangible situations (goals, objectives, time frames) than an emotional state of mind. To put undue pressure on yourself that tomorrow or next week you will feel this way or that way is wasted energy, and that energy should be spent focusing on what you can accomplish today.

First things first

Take care of what *you* need to do first. Complete it to the best of your ability before you move on to the next task. Whether it is physical or psychological, keep it in its proper order of importance—it can be as simple as making your bed before you start your day, or making sure your loved one is genuinely seeking help before you offer your services.

Let go and let God

This slogan is probably the most difficult for many people to capture. You have to first believe in a higher power with a fair amount of fortitude and confidence, and then be able to turn your will and care over to that higher power or the God of your understanding. To let go of the control over the uncertainty and upheaval of your life and trust that your higher power will take care of you is very difficult; especially when that control might involve the alcoholic / addict. I find comfort in the idea that God is my copilot or my silent partner, and that he has me exactly where I'm supposed to be at this time and in this place. The challenge comes when we don't like, or are uncomfortable with, what we are facing. We hold on so tight to what we want to have, or think we should have, that we sabotage the ability to *let go of our way of thinking and turn our will and care over to our higher power.* Prayer can help you to find peace in your decision. If you look back, you will find many things you experienced with difficulty that somehow, against all odds, worked out, even if it wasn't the way you had hoped or thought.

Easy does it

Life can be interesting and complicated. Loving and dealing with the alcoholic / addict makes life even more dramatic and mercurial. If you can, try to be gentle with yourself. Physical, emotional, or psychological efforts should be handled with a tender approach. Don't flog yourself or beat yourself up for what you think you should or shouldn't have done for another because of their addiction struggles. Negative judgment is not welcome here.

One day at a time

Much like *Just for today*, the phrase *One day at a time* is exactly that: take one day at a time and work through the challenges presented on that day and only that day. One day at a time is the only way you can deal with life or your loved one's addiction, whether in recovery or not.

Keep an open mind

To me, this slogan is paramount in my daily life. If I can keep an open mind, then I can allow for unexpected circumstances or situations to arise. Years ago, I went to hear Jack Canfield speak. A gifted orator and the author of the *Chicken Soup for the Soul* books, he showed the audience a video of people passing a basketball between them. He instructed us to keep count of how many times the ball was passed from person to person. About halfway through the video a man in a gorilla suit appeared and stood in front of the camera waving. When the lights came on, he asked how many people saw the man in the gorilla suit? Although we had been instructed to keep a close watch on the bouncing of the ball he reminded us of the importance of keeping an open mind for unexpected possibilities that might change the path of thinking upon which we were so determined. Don't be so hell-bent on the task at hand that you miss other opportunities that may prove beneficial if you take the time to see them and keep an open mind in the process.

Let it begin with me

It's easy to point the finger regarding our unhappiness, and thereby blame our discontent on others. But if we first look at ourselves and what we need to change in attitude, expectations, or communication, then we can start to be satisfied in our own recovery process. A healthy self is important in being clearheaded and grounded when dealing with the alcoholic / addict.

Listen and learn

Keeping quiet is very difficult for me. I want to interject, defend, or justify my viewpoint as often as possible. Listening is a gift, and though one may not agree with, or even like, what they are hearing, there may be something to be learned at the end of the exchange. Even if what you have learned is sad and difficult, like realizing that a relationship is over, you have still learned something.

Keep it simple

A parallel slogan to *Easy does it*, keeping things simple will help you maintain your actions and life choices. Sometimes the answer is very obvious and doesn't need to be evaluated or dissected dozens of ways for the same outcome. There is no need to make things so convoluted that you get twisted up trying to find an answer; it might be right in front of your nose.

Live and let live

Taking another's inventory about how they are running their life, spending their money, or raising their children is out of line, disrespectful, and rude. Many relationships have terminated because one person does not allow the other to live the life they want. Everybody has an opinion. Family members can have a field day advising or lecturing to other family members what they should or should not do about relationships, jobs, money, and child rearing. Allow people to live their own lives; if they ask for help, great, but otherwise, zip it.

My Own Personal Slogans and Mantras

Here are some slogans/mantras that I have formulated myself or heard from others. As I believe you can never have too many words of positive infusion, I have listed them to share with you. You can pick and choose as you like.

Working toward better days ahead

I discussed this in a previous chapter, but I feel another look can't hurt. My true daily mantra expresses no pressure towards how much work I should be doing and places no expectations on my specific definition of "better days." This mantra allows me to quell my busy brain and appreciate that I am working toward better days. I feel confident that they are ahead; just be patient and keep on truckin'. Keeping my eye on what's ahead, my goals, plans, and passions will allow those better days to unfold; even if it's slower than a snail.

Do the footwork and let the game come to you

Sometimes all you can do is what's in front of you. Doing the footwork to write a book, filling out job applications, completing an exercise program, or even online dating is about "suiting up and showing up." Doing the footwork, and then allowing the game to unfold as it might, takes you and your futile idea of control out of the results.

God helps people that help themselves

This comes from my father who would tell me this when I was facing a difficult task. I was taught that nothing comes easily or for nothing, and that hard work pays off. "Helping oneself" is subject to different definitions, so just stick to the one you are comfortable with. Also, don't expect "God" to help you the way you want just because you feel that you have kept up your end of the bargain. A higher power works in mysterious ways and may help us in those ways that we have not even considered. We simply have put our best, most honest, and healthiest work out there; I strongly believe that the work will not be ignored. Do the task that's in front of you, keep your head high and eyes forward, and this dedication will not be ignored.

He brought me to it, he'll lead me through it

For me, this is a warm and fuzzy slogan. I believe in God and a strong spirituality factor, and like the slogan *Let go and let God* I believe that if my higher power has brought me to a particularly difficult time in my life, he will not abandon me. Hence, if he brought me to it, there was a reason, and he will lead me through even if it's painful and scary. I will come out the other end stronger, wiser, more accepting, loving, empathetic, forgiving ... hey, the list can and should go on and on.

Every breath is healing

When we breathe, our bodies relax. Breathing can be like a discrete, tiny tranquilizer and calm us down to regroup, reorganize, and dig deeper for mental or emotional strength. A kissing cousin to hitting the pause button, you need to breathe in order to hit that button. One cannot be effective without the other. We utilize only a portion of our lungs when we breathe by habit, so take the time for a deep, fulfilling breath of delicious air and enjoy the healing, relaxing experience.

I'm doing the best I can

Even if you have done nothing that day besides stay in bed and cry, you are doing the best you can for that day with the tools you have. Please don't beat yourself up if you are hoping to, or expected to—yet unable to—move mountains, plan a vacation, or have a decent discussion with the alcoholic / addict. When you hit the pillow that night, tell yourself that you did the best you could for that day. If you feel that you might have done a tad better, tomorrow is another day, and you can attack it from a fresh approach and perspective.

Stay on course

Even if you feel that the walls are closing in on you, stay on your course. In my troubled times, I found that writing this book epitomized staying on course. It represented a boat navigating through choppy, dark, and uncertain waters. My crew was my family, friends, and pets. I found that if I stayed on my personal course, eyes ahead, the fireballs, dragons, monsters, and all other forms of evil could not harm me. I often found myself saying, "Today, I will stay on course, regardless of what is thrown in my path."

I hope you find some of these helpful. Select a few phrases that particularly hit home and place them in strategic spots around your house, office, or car. I have found such mantras to be a small shot of mental or emotional adrenaline. Think about them as needed; you might find that you have built your own verbal defense system.

To love oneself is the beginning of a lifelong romance.
OSCAR WILDE

Chapter 16

WHEN IS IT TIME
TO THROW IN THE TOWEL?

Deciding to walk away from a relationship usually is a painful, gut-wrenching decision. In a conventional scenario, ending a relationship can be difficult enough, but add in a strong contributing factor of substance abuse, and there can be heartache, fear, uncertainty, and guilt as well. With an addiction landscape, there may come a time when you feel that you have exhausted all of your avenues in trying to live with the alcoholic / addict—and your own personal well being is now in danger. Whether your loved one is in their full-blown addiction or in physical recovery but continues a disposition of the dry drunk, you may find that you have run out of gas, and you may see that the only healthy option is to throw in the towel and make a dramatic, earthshaking move.

Like the alcoholic / addict who may hit bottom before realizing that it's time to change the course that their life is on, or die, the family member or friend can hit bottom as well. This decision may come from a place of anger or from days and months of gut-wrenching indecision. Either way, you have probably shed buckets of tears and can't believe that your life has come to this fork in the road.

I know that when I was considering leaving my husband, I spent what seemed to be a decade of sleepless nights pondering my decision. After all, regardless of his alcoholic behavior, I did love the man and we had a family, and after twenty years we had built a life together. But, deep down I couldn't shake the itch that told me I had to bail. I didn't know who I was anymore. Like someone drowning, I desperately needed to grab onto any piece of wood that might allow me to reclaim my life. His addiction brought out the worst in me. I was quick to anger, brittle, and paranoid about my decisions. Who was I? What had I become? I had lost friends, and family members didn't like being around me. Finally, I believed it had to be better in the long run for myself and my family that I end the marriage even with the excruciating pain that I knew would accompany my decision. I kept in mind that the big picture of making a new life for myself had to outweigh the almost impossibility that maybe tomorrow would be different if I stayed. I had been down that disappointing road so many times before that I found it helpful to burn those memories in my head; I knew I would call upon them in the future when I felt shaky about my decision. With all this said, here are a number of reasons why you might stay longer in a relationship with the alcoholic/addict than maybe you should:

1. Gripped with fear as to what your life will become
2. Feeling that children are better off with two parents rather than one, regardless of the discomfort and tension in the household
3. The alcoholic/addict is the chief money maker and you would be left financially compromised
4. Fear of retribution
5. Fear of being alone
6. Hanging on to the few shreds of normal behavior that the alcoholic/addict randomly shows (and hoping one day soon it will stick)
7. Social, family (extended or otherwise), and peer pressure that you should keep trying to stick it out
8. Believing that things will change if you "do this" or "do that"
9. The confusion of "what went wrong?" or "what happened?—It used to be so good," and difficulty in facing a new harsh reality
10. Embarrassed, ashamed, and somehow feeling guilty
11. Worrying about what people will say: gossip
12. Honoring commitments; feeling religious constraints
13. Poor reflection on self and self-esteem
14. Fearful that the alcoholic/addict may relapse, disappear, or commit suicide

I experienced almost all of these mental land mines. Some days I would be gripped with fear about what might happen to my loved one, the alcoholic / addict, if I were to end our marriage; other days, I would be focused on my children or my fear of being alone. Yet, for every reason that I found myself staying, I wrote down healthy reasons for me to make that difficult but life-saving decision. Are any of these reasons formulating in your head?

1. You are mentally and physically exhausted in dealing with the out-of-control behavior of the alcoholic / addict.
2. Whether in their addictive state or displaying the brittle, annoyed, resentful, angry disposition of the dry drunk, you sadly don't like this person anymore. What happened to that man or woman you fell in love with?
3. You can no longer trust what they say or do.
4. The bullying behavior, as they circumvent their own problems on to you, and the constant ridicule have left you wondering what happened to who and what you were and taken your confidence to an all-time low.
5. You are weary of the constant merry-go-round of rehabilitation attempts that don't seem to stick for long.
6. You are embarrassed that you don't think better of yourself. You are actually ashamed that you have let this get as far as it has.
7. You are no longer fearful of being alone, since you realize that your loved one is already living a life apart from you with their drug of choice.
8. Everyone's world is revolving around the alcoholic / addict and consequently your family is suffering.
9. You are fearful of any discussions as they are always combative and disrespectful. Therefore, you can't walk over any more eggshells in your effort to keep them from anger.
10. No matter how hard you try, the alcoholic / addict keeps raising the bar for you to "do your part" in the relationship; satisfaction is never reached.
11. The thought of spending one more minute of your life like this is physically making you ill.
12. You no longer care how it looks to others, what anyone says, or what the ramifications may be of your decision.

13. The negative energy permeating from the alcoholic / addict hangs
like a dense fog around your house and you are suffocating in it.

No matter what your reasons, whether they are listed above or not,
you have hit your bottom and are ready to take the painful but appropriate
step to move on with your life without the alcoholic / addict. Please don't
beat yourself if you are distressed that you have not acted on this resolve
sooner. It is very hard to blow out the candle in the window that you
think represents hope, but realistically doesn't represent that. People stay
in unhealthy relationships for a myriad of reasons, and no one has the right
to judge another's decisions. Unless you walk in another's shoes, or know
what goes on behind closed doors, your decision is yours and yours alone
and does not need the approval or disapproval of anyone.

It is substantially more difficult to walk away from your child regardless of their age. These can be uncertain and difficult years just because of
where they are in the sphere of adulthood, and parents want to be there for
their children to offer advice and instill encouragement. However, having
one foot in childhood and one foot in the independent world of adulthood doesn't change the accountability and responsibility of this young
person for their decisions. If there is an addiction issue, the majority of
parents still cannot abandon or walk away from their child, but instead, it's
important to present very strong boundaries to be followed or else certain
ramifications may be enforced: like no financial support, questionable college attendance, or living at home no longer being an option.

My client Chuck has been involved with his adult child through her
many rehabilitation attempts. His daughter lost everything due to her addiction: a powerful job, beautiful home, and caring friends. Her father
stood by her side through bankruptcy and living on the streets and continued to encourage her desire to rehabilitate her life. After eighteen months
of successful clean and sober living, Chuck's daughter had yet another relapse. Sadly, her father felt no other option but to throw in the towel.
Chuck told her that he loved her and would pray for her daily, but he had
to disengage all communication and physical contact with her until she
had logged a substantial amount of clean and sober time under her belt.

Detaching from a parent, sibling, or friend can be difficult, but if they
are not a daily focal point of your life (like a spouse or child), it might be
easier. What usually stops us from walking away from an abusive parent is
guilt. After all, this is your mother or father, and even the Ten Command-

ments say we should honor our parents. But at what price? If these people make your blood pressure rise, or give you a stomachache with the mere mention of their name, then please rethink why you are in this relationship. If you can't throw in the towel, then think about "if you can't beat 'em, join 'em." This doesn't mean that you allow them to walk all over you or make mincemeat of your insides, just know what to expect when dealing with them. Approach them with a "yeah … whatever" attitude. Limit your visits or phone participation; literally, put a time frame on these and tell them that you can only be involved with them for "x" amount of minutes, hours, or God forbid, days. If you can implement this, you have thrown in the towel; even though it's the size of a washcloth, it comes with respect and dignity from your end.

Remember your boundaries; don't be afraid to state that if they say this or that, or do this or that, then you will have to excuse yourself since you will be uncomfortable with the exchange or setting.

Though difficult, please try and remember that a few years of discomfort, uncertainty, and fear are better than years and years of an agonizing and miserable commitment. Some may feel that they are a failure if they abandon their relationship. Coming to this conclusion and realizing that the end is upon you can actually be incredibly empowering. Take some comfort in knowing that you have taken control of the situation. Sometimes it's the bravest option since it requires you to face what you might think of as a failure. But it is not a failure. In life, there really is no such thing as a crash-and-burn scenario; there are only lessons to be learned for a better, healthier go around the next time.

Before sunlight can shine through a window,
the blinds must be raised.
AMERICAN PROVERB

Section Four

RELAPSE
AND RECOVERY

This section focuses back on the alcoholic / addict. The recovery plan or contract is very important; it puts into action everything we have discussed thus far in regard to you and your loved one. Your confidence with communication and boundaries will now be put to the test.

Chapter 17

THE FAMILY RECOVERY PLAN OR CONTRACT

After the hard work you have done processing and implementing the recommendations in this book, all will be for naught if you have no recovery plan or contract! A recovery plan or contract is just that: a plan or contract for those in recovery and those closely associated with their loved one's recovery. Its purpose is to present realistic goals and subsequent consequences that both the family member or friend and the alcoholic / addict can live with whether successful in those goals or not.

It is the irresponsible parent, spouse, mate, family member, or friend who does not insist upon a structure or plan, but instead hopes that everything will work out okay or hopes that a few well intended ideas from the alcoholic / addict will suffice.

You may start out with very good and clear intentions of what you expect from them as they begin to put their life back together, but we all struggle and are uncomfortable with what to do next if those goals or expectations are not met. It's so much easier to be the good guy then the bad guy, and punishment or ramifications can so easily take a back seat to the recovery plan or contract as you might think, "Well, things are going so well. I don't want to rock the boat, and let's just cross that bridge when we come to it." This is a terrible mistake if your intentions aren't clear right from the beginning. You stand on very shaky ground if you think that you have any power to implement anything while your loved one serves up a plethora of excuses, ignores you, or walks out the door.

I have heard many clients say that once their son or daughter returned to live at home after being involved in a recovery program, the family requested or even demanded that their loved one keep their room clean, help with the household chores, return to school, or get a job. The loved one agreed, but after a while things slacked off, family and friends got busy, or life was rolling along and everyone became complacent. When this occurred, I would ask my clients what happened to the consequence column.

While you don't want to be a babysitter to your loved one, if they are living under your roof, then they must live within your guidelines.

Later in this chapter, I'm going to elaborate on the components of a recovery plan or contract specifically designed for a child (using this term generically to describe ages up to eighteen or twenty-one) still under the umbrella of the immediate family. Then I'm going to show you how to adapt this plan or contract for a mate/spouse or other close relationships. As long as the alcoholic/addict is in recovery and your life is involved with theirs, the recovery plan or contract represents important boundaries and guidelines that will help to develop respect between you and them.

It is important to tackle this recovery plan or contract together and in writing. However, with that said, the alcoholic/addict needs to put together what they see as their recovery plan or contract first! Don't allow them to be lazy and say, "Whatever you want is fine with me." That's B.S. and a cop-out on their part. The alcoholic/addict is afforded no privileges UNTIL a recovery plan or contract is in place. Make yourself available once they have come to you and said that they are ready to sit down and discuss their thinking on how they see their responsibilities AND consequences if they are not carried out.

When you are sitting together and they state that they want or need to get a job or do volunteer work, then have them write down *how* they see this happening, (Internet, personally going into establishments, cold calling, networking), *when* they think this can be accomplished, (ten days, two weeks, one month), and *what* they think are reasonable consequences (financial support suspended, cell phone taken away, computer rights denied, or entertainment plans postponed) if they don't fulfill this aspect of their recovery plan or contract.

Be careful about being too vague, both for you and the alcoholic/addict. For example, let's say you want to implement the requirement that the your loved one be home at a reasonable hour; to do this you need to pinpoint a specific time, don't just leave it to a last minute decision or whatever your loved one thinks is reasonable. Here are other examples of identifying specific goals: keeping their room neat—does this mean white glove cleanliness or just clothes off the floor?; taking out the garbage— what night and what time?; walking the dog—how many times a day and how many days a week?; preparing or cleaning up meals—which meals and how often?

Anything that fits with your family routine should be part of the recovery plan. Be specific; leave nothing to interpretation!

I advise my clients to pick the following four areas to start the recovery plan or contract with, as these should be obvious and natural skill sets:

1. **Remain clean and sober.** This can be difficult to implement, but relying on instinct to decide whether or not your loved one has been drinking or using drugs is a lot of babysitting for you and can result in engagement, a non-neutral posture, and resentment on both your ends. Remember that the first "rule" is to abstain from ANY AND ALL mind-altering substance. Are you really that good at detecting even one drink or one hit of marijuana? Don't put yourself in the position of judge and jury; hence, random drug testing is a healthy and acceptable option. If your loved one has nothing to hide, they will only be too happy to comply. Find a drug-testing center that has the proper equipment for ensuring reliable testing and results. Please don't do this yourself as you should not be too personally involved in this part of the recovery process. Anyway, the alcoholic / addict has to urinate in a cup and someone has to witness a clean specimen, and I don't think you want to participate in that. Also, remember that I said *all* mind-altering substance. Be aware that your loved one may try to convince you that since alcohol was not their drug of choice, it's not a problem, or that a few lines of cocaine shouldn't be an issue since alcohol was their drug of choice. If your loved one is taking prescription medication, please consult with their physician to tell them of your loved one's recovery program and to determine if there is an alternative to addictive medication.

2. **Attend AA Twelve Step recovery meetings; see a professional addiction counselor.** My recommendation is at least three Twelve Step recovery meetings a week (their presence will be confirmed

by the signing of their "meeting card" at the conclusion of the meeting by the secretary of that meeting) and a meeting with a substance abuse counselor at least once a week initially and then every other week if recovery is going smoothly. Remember that the Twelve Step recovery meetings are for remaining clean and sober and appreciating the experience of others, and the counseling is for the emotional and psychological baggage from addiction as well as for learning to live life on life's terms.

3. **Engage in employment or volunteer work.** Thirty to forty hours a week keeping busy and responsible is a vital part of any recovery plan or contract. Chances are the alcoholic/addict has been on a rigid schedule if they are involved in almost any kind of rehabilitation program. Keeping busy and accountable to themselves and others can be a strong tether in avoiding relapse. Knowing what is expected, to whom, what time, and where are simple, basic structures that they can start to build confidence with. It is preferable that the alcoholic/addict find paying employment versus volunteer work. It's obvious that there is more responsibility attached to their commitment if they are getting paid than being able to call in sick or not show up for a volunteer position where there is no ramification. However, anything that the alcoholic/addict does that gets them out of the house and clocking in responsible hours is an excellent start to any program or contract.

4. **Participate within the family unit.** It's important for your loved one to demonstrate their desire to become part of the family unit or structure again, and it's important for the family to start accepting them again as well. Regaining their credibility and re-igniting the love and trust that were probably lost during the addictive years are critical in the reconstruction years. Start small, as you don't want to overwhelm or push too hard. Yet, a Sunday meal or weekend movie should be doable as well as something to look forward to by all.

If any of the above commitments (or others that you choose) are not met with the understanding that you both have agreed to follow already, then without hesitation, be dedicated to implementing the consequences that were spelled out in the recovery plan or contract.

If your loved one has completed a residential recovery program, such a contract might not take effect until the program is completed. (Please don't allow the alcoholic/addict to convince you that this recovery program is not for them or that they have learned as much as they can, therefore, they are leaving. This is irresponsible thinking and calls into question their commitment to sobriety) Once they return home or to a sober living house, your involvement will certainly be different than it was previously. Have a confirmed date to discuss the treatment plan or contract before the program is over. This way everyone can be on the same page after graduation, and if need be the residential treatment counselor can help you and your loved one navigate through any communication hiccups.

Conversely, if your loved one is not going to have any involvement with friends or family and is planning to continue recovery independently, or opt out of recovery altogether, then no recovery contract is needed. But keep in mind that even the slightest involvement would be more likely to have a positive result if a written or strongly stated understanding is in place.

For example, if the only involvement with the family is an occasional meal, then make sure the expected time and conditions are clearly stated. Tell your loved one that you require a clean and sober dinner companion. Both excessive tardiness and questionable sobriety constitute reasons to scratch the whole evening.

All the honest and hard-earned work that has been done to reach this place of recovery for both of you needs the framework of an agreed-upon plan if you are both to keep grounded and focused. Implementing consequences if your loved one does not meet their goals or commitments is crucial to the success of the recovery plan or contract.

The following are important aspects of the recovery plan or contract:

1. Represents a routine for the alcoholic/addict
2. Offers a tangible doable outline of behavior with achievable goals; your loved one will come to respect and appreciate the rules and regulations of this agreement.
3. Allows for the alcoholic/addict to rebuild their life in a safe, supportive, and nonjudgmental environment
4. Allows for the family members and/or friends to rebuild their trust in their loved one in a safe, supportive, and nonjudgmental environment

5. Clarifies for everyone involved what is expected from the alcoholic / addict and the consequences if these expectations are not met

I have discussed a very specific recovery plan or contract, but maybe it's too convoluted or difficult for you to implement. My client Sharon felt that way regarding her lack of stick-to-itiveness with her son who was coming out of a three-month residential rehabilitation program. Sharon tried unsuccessfully to insist that her son go to a sober living house for six months instead of sharing an apartment with a buddy. She wasn't happy about his decision but felt that she couldn't just abandon him and let him flounder financially. Together we constructed a recovery plan/contract that looked like this:

- Sharon would pay for the first month's apartment rent in full.
- Sharon would pay for one-half of the second month's apartment rent.
- Sharon would pay for one-quarter of the third month's apartment rent.
- Sharon's son would be available for random drug testing during this three-month period at an established facility.

If her son could not come up with the remainder of the rent after the first month, Sharon would not augment the difference. If her son tested positive for drugs at any time during the three months, then the contract was null and void. If any of these were to occur, she would only pay the rent at a sober living home and no place else.

Sharon felt comfortable with this plan and confident that she could enforce it. This was the key for her, as it is important to remember that we all are different and our fiber for implementing the consequences varies from person to person.

I instructed Sharon (as I do all my clients) to sleep on her contract/ recovery plan—the rules, regulations, and consequences. What might empower a client in my office may be uncertain or flimsy when the dust settles.

Remember, let your loved one come up with their idea of recovery and personal commitments and consequences first. It allows them to be a major participant of the agreement and accountable for the outcome—whether it is ultimately all their plan, a combination of yours and theirs, or all yours. It's great if at the end of the day there has been a healthy and amicable negotiation between the two or you (or more family partici-pants). This way everyone can feel like they have worked hard to be heard and their ideas can be incorporated as a partnership and not a dictatorship.

Rewards

Before I move on to the spouse or partner, let's take a minute to talk about rewards. Rewards seem to be more relevant to children and their addiction issues than to adults. Parents often feel that they need to reward (or want to reward) their children for good behavior. I am all for reward-ing honest, healthy actions, but keep in mind that the real reward should be a clean and sober lifestyle and all the riches that come with that. If you wish to reward your child with something tangible, let's look at a couple of options that may be fulfilling for both of you and are not just the carrot at the end of the stick for being a good boy or girl and doing the right thing.

One idea might be to plan a family vacation. Maybe pick somewhere that your loved one has never been and has always had a desire to visit. Depending on your finances and interest, anything from a camping trip to a Mediterranean cruise could be rewarding. While planning it together as a family, there is nothing wrong with discussing some fair boundaries and expectations that you all agree upon. (These may have nothing to do with staying clean and sober but may pertain to the normal, everyday expecta-tions of a family.)

Some parents wish to purchase a car for their child or fund a number of months in an apartment to demonstrate their vote of confidence in their child's budding sobriety. Again, these well-meaning parents might feel that a reward is definitely in order since their son or daughter has gone through such a difficult period and has come out on the other side with flying col-ors. After all, children are frequently rewarded for good grades in school, so why not reward them for getting clean and sober? In my experience this is not a healthy, productive way of thinking.

However, if you are hell-bent on rewarding your child in a big way, please wait at least one year to eighteen months before you plunk down thousands of dollars for something. This way they can prove not only to you, but to themselves as well, that they are C.A.R.D. (credible, account-able, responsible, and dependable).

Truth be told, I'm leery about making huge investments unless there is some fiscal responsibility held by the person in recovery. For example, let's look at the responsibility attached to rewarding with a car. First, both you and your loved one should discuss your views and expectations about the purchase. Maybe you each agree to pay for one-half the purchase cost. (This is a promising goal for the person in recovery to work toward, but it may take a year or two). Second, maybe your loved one pays for insurance, gas, and maintenance. The point is to expect some accountability not only to you but personal accountability to themselves as well.

If you agree on some financial plan but your loved one doesn't have the money for gas or insurance, please don't cover these expenses in the hope that you will be paid back. Parents have a way of forgetting or letting things slide to be the "good guys" so that their children will like them more. Don't forget to incorporate whatever ramifications both of you come up with if a car payment (or whatever is agreed upon) is not remitted on time. A person in addiction recovery will function best when they know very clearly what the rules of the game are and what is expected.

One last thought: It's so desperately hard not to do whatever it takes to help our children find their way out of the dark pit of substance abuse. I know that as I tried for years—and still do. With that said, many of my clients have come to me confident in some ways, yet more confused than ever about certain aspects of their recovery plan or contract with their children. For example:

- Can I pay for counseling for my child?
- How long should I let them live at home?
- Should I pay for education?
- Should I pay for another rehabilitation program if there is a relapse?

The answer to all of these is, "yes and no." If there is genuine commitment and progress being made in counseling, then yes. You might allow your child to live at home until they have six months of income put away to then either rent their own apartment or pay you some rent. Should you pay for education? Absolutely, but demand to see grades, and pay for the education directly to the school and not to your child. Rehab? That's a tough one. If this is the third or fourth attempt, then seek advice from a professional; If it's a genuine desire to pick themselves up after a relapse, consider it. Take some time to discuss with your loved one what went wrong and what will be different in the future if you invest in another rehabilitation program. You don't want your child to make it a career going to rehab programs and using that as an excuse instead of implementing what they have learned in recovery.

The bottom line is that you have to use your own best judgment. Clearly and honestly step back and look at the whole picture. How much is committed action for the betterment of themselves, and how much is smoke and mirrors? If you can really be unbiased, the answer will come to you. And put a time cap on things. Pay for counseling for six months then regroup with your loved one to see what they are gaining and if they want to continue what might be a payment plan. How long will they live at home, and what is their payment responsibility?

Having your loved one invested in their own life provides a sense of accomplishment and purpose. It can be a wonderful experience for everyone to share in the pride and participate in the growth and development of their beloved recovering individual.

Recovery Plan or Contract for a Mate or Spouse

Obviously, the most important element to any recovery plan or contract is remaining clean and sober. Without living a clean and sober lifestyle, everything else is pointless. Beyond that, the aspects of the recovery plan or contract that are paramount to its success are whatever you and your mate or spouse establish as personal goals between you. For example, these goals might be attending couple's counseling, finding new activities to do together, and developing new friendships.

I have encouraged my adult clients who are working at a clean and sober program to find something that they can be passionate about. Returning to school to get a higher degree or physical activities like sailing, tennis, or bicycling can fit the bill. Hobbies are an excellent way to keep the mind creative and occupied—painting, wood working, or building anything from model airplanes to old cars. A suitable alternative can be anything that breaks the old cycle that had drinking or drugs a main part of the routine.

Regardless of the recovery plan or contract being for your child or for your mate or spouse, consequences are still a part of the agreement. If the alcoholic/addict does not fulfill their end of the bargain, from remaining clean and sober to attending counseling with you (or whatever the two of you have agreed upon) then you might find yourself taking some time away from home—this might be a few hours at a movie, an overnight out of the house, or a few months living somewhere else. This time away is used as a re-evaluation period for you as well. The difference between this contract or recovery plan and that for a child is that if the child does not follow through on their commitment, the consequence is placed upon them, such as losing their cell phone privileges, shortened curfew, or returning to a professional treatment center or school. With an adult, since you can't punish them, you have to take the initiative to take care of yourself; your mate or spouse will undoubtedly be affected by the decisions you make.

Recovery Contract Case Study

Though not a recovery plan, this is a proposed contract my client Oscar presented to his mate as he was concerned about her alcohol intake. It was clear that they were going their separate ways, yet they had two small children together, and Oscar was concerned about their well being.

Rita (the mother of the children) had multiple DUIs and Oscar felt she was often irresponsible regarding the care and attention of their children. Oscar had tried several times to discuss his concerns not only about her drinking but about the welfare of the children, yet he reported that Rita constantly turned a deaf ear, often retreating to family or friends as a refuge. Oscar had hit a brick wall and now felt that his only option was to give Rita certain ultimatums or get the law involved. Oscar drafted a proposal to give to Rita. With his permission, I am offering it here.

Rita and Oscar's Separation Proposal
Plan during the summer while I begin a Miami apartment search:

1. During the week, there will be three days in a row with the children for me and three days in a row for Rita. The days in which Rita has the children can be spent at the house if she chooses, but I can be there also if I would like. Rita can be there during my time as well. One day a week, Rita and I could attempt to do something with the children together.
2. Rita will keep me apprised as to any significant decisions made regarding the children (schools, medical, etc.).
3. I can take the children to see my friends and family during my

three days at my discretion.

4. Rita and I will work together to come up with a short-term financial plan, as I will continue to support her and the children as she looks for work.

5. Rita and I will work together to come up with a plan regarding the pets and where they will live.

6. Rita and I will work out a plan regarding the use of the car including the eventual transfer of title as she does not currently have legal driving privileges.

7. I will be responsible for the maintenance of the house as well as putting it up for sale.

8. Rita and I will discuss the possibility of the children living with me in Miami and going to private preschool and kindergarten this fall.

9. Anytime when Rita has the children and I am not around, she will communicate with me that she is awake by at least 9:00 a.m.

So, how does Oscar's proposal shake out? While trying to be non-combative and friendly, Oscar is giving, or allowing, Rita to have all the power or say in each decision. In addition, it is very vague, as I sense that Oscar does not want to anger or incite Rita. He is tippy-toeing around what is important to him and hoping she will agree. In essence, though he has stated his desires, he has left it totally up to her to approve or not. This agreement also lacks brackets or time frames.

Here is the proposal I drafted for him, which still incorporates his wishes but has some confidence and clarity:

Rita,

It is important to me that we have a clear and precise understanding regarding the disposition of our children and their visitation rights with us both. I have put together an informal proposal that I think is fair and equitable.

We have two wonderful children together and they are innocent as to issues between us. They deserve both of our love and attention as caring and responsible parents and adults; I know that you would not disagree.

After careful thought, I have listed what is fair from a financial obligation as well as parental rights.

I will have the children three days a week unencumbered, and you will have them three days a week. On the seventh day, we will use our best efforts to share the company of our children jointly. In the event that is not possible for whatever reason, then we will rotate the fourth day between us every other week.

Neither one of us may make significant decisions regarding school, vacations, living situations, medical issues, or other important decisions without discussing and obtaining the approval of the other prior to the intended date.

I will support you and the children with $_____ per month for four months as you continue to look for employment. Beyond the four months, we will revisit the financial issue again and the status of your employment. I will however continue to support the children at $_____ for the next _____ years before revisiting their financial needs.

I will be responsible for the maintenance of the house and spearheading the sale of the house at a mutually acceptable date. The proceeds from the sale of the house, outstanding debts and taxes will be _____ (whatever is worked out or due).

Miscellaneous issues like our mutual pets and other important yet not imperative issues will be discussed and concluded in a reasonable, respectful, and timely manner agreed to by both of us.

I am concerned about your alcohol intake. Though it is none of my business if you drink or not, it is my concern if it involves our children and their well being. If I don't hear from you by 9:00 a.m. on the days that you have the children, I will come and get them. The last thing I want is to get child welfare services or the police involved, but as a concerned parent I will have no option but to do whatever the safest, healthiest, and proper steps are to ensure our children's best interest.

Rita, as I stated in the beginning, I know you and I both want what's best for our children. This agreement is not about taking pot shots at you, but about being responsible parents and at the same time respecting each other.

Oscar

It is highly unlikely that Rita will accept this proposal with open arms. She may be angry and combative as things are not as they have always been, and now she may be faced for the first time with accountability for her actions. In turn, Oscar is finally working at his boundaries and the consequences if Rita doesn't agree. Rita may not agree, but her option is to then put together a counterproposal as to what she is willing or not willing to do. They can choose to go back and forth in good faith until an understanding is reached, or Oscar can present a take-it-or-leave-it posture or get the law involved.

Unlike the other recovery plans that I talked about previously (other than coming to pick up the children if Rita does not answer the phone by 9:00 am), there is nothing stated or written for consequences. I didn't feel it important to come to the table with all barrels loaded with ammo, as this is the first attempt to come to an amicable, respectful agreement between two people. Consequences can be presented as a plan B if Rita ignores or disregards the proposal. Oscar can take the time to contemplate his options or research his legal rights if this proposal (or any agreement that is not followed) blows up in his face.

The important concept to remember in this chapter is that any agreement or understanding can be deemed a recovery plan or contract when it is between two people where substance abuse has played a factor in poor choices or out-of-control behavior. Since so much of the alcoholic / addict's behavior has been unreliable or duplicitous, it is the responsible parent, spouse, mate, sibling, friend, or co-worker who should insist that a written document represents a true and clear understanding of what is expected from both parties. Think of it as a guardrail on the freeway keeping you and your car safe from swerving off the intended path.

What we learn to do, we learn by doing.
ARISTOTLE

Chapter 18

IS RELAPSE PART OF RECOVERY?

Is relapse part of recovery? As an addiction counselor, I am asked this question all the time. My answer is both "yes" and "no," depending on whom you are talking about and their experiences. If one has relapsed, learned from their slip, and embraced a stronger, more committed recovery, then the answer is "yes." However, if one continues to relapse because they are not tethered to working a clean and sober lifestyle, then relapse is in effect an excuse for buying more time while deciding whether to commit to sobriety. Hence, the answer for this individual is "no."

Some alcoholic/addicts embrace a clean and sober lifestyle from the day they commit to it. That said, the majority experience some hiccups along the way. Relapse can occur when the alcoholic/addict has still not thoroughly committed to the mindset that substance abuse is not an option in their life. They may be experiencing more than enough support and help through Twelve Step meetings, sponsorship, and even private or group counseling, but their own personal determination is missing. Without all of these elements (and maybe even more) working together like a well-oiled machine, the alcoholic/addict could have a more difficult road toward sobriety and white knuckling it more than necessary.

Four Main Dispositions of Relapse

For the person addicted to alcohol or other drugs who is committed to, and working on, a recovery program, I have found that there are four main dispositions that present formidable challenges and can potentially trigger relapse. In chapter 19, I discuss seventy-seven (yes, you read it right,

77!) warning signs of relapse. Here, I offer the four strongest emotional challenges for the alcoholic / addict; these factors contribute greatly to relapse and require detailed discussion.

Relapse is an individual preference depending on the circumstances that trigger that relapse. However, remember that a relapse is a relapse even if the drug of choice is cocaine and the relapse is with alcohol. In addition, whether it is one toke of a joint or a weeklong drinking binge, I still consider both a relapse. Yet, the severity of the relapse differs greatly and might be taken into consideration. Obviously, a weeklong bender is more destructive than a few hits of a joint.

The four factors that I discuss here might represent kryptonite to some people in recovery, regardless of how long they've been sober or how strong their program. In addition, remember that maybe one or more of these four dispositions might have been a major contributor to their original route to addiction in the first place.

- Expectation
- Resentment
- Boredom
- Fear

Expectation

Falling short of expectations or the feeling that the alcoholic / addict is unable to fulfill what is expected can open the floodgates to relapse. Whether it is your expectations as a friend or family member or the expectations of the alcoholic / addict, expectations can become unrealistic. After all, your loved one can get swept up with that initial fast or easy recovery. An early sense of comfort and lack of physical or emotional challenge is a honeymoon period that often falsely revolves around a happy work environment or a fairy-tale relationship. Expectations seem fulfilled at this stage, yet when the initial glow of that honeymoon subsides and reality's imperfections set in, your loved one might not know how to deal with the frustration or disappointment; hence, they may turn back to the only way they know to ensure comfort: getting high or intoxicated.

I talked about your expectations in chapter 9, but it is crucial for the alcoholic / addict to keep a watchful eye on their expectations as well. If your loved one can keep their expectations healthy, and in check, the chance of relapse (because their expectations were too lofty or unrealistic) may not present such formidable odds. Remember that the alcoholic/addict may take on Herculean tasks in an effort to prove to themselves and others how smart, strong, or good they are—or in an attempt to make up lost time due to their addiction. Hence, they might not be able to help themselves, but to overextend in unrealistic expectations. If the expectation falls short, the alcoholic/addict may have trouble taking this failure in stride. Therefore, they may revert to the opposite end of the spectrum and find themselves saying, "Screw it, I can't do anything right, so why not have a couple of snorts or belts." Falling short of expectations is a very prevalent and strong disposition for relapse.

Resentment

When the alcoholic/addict has pent up resentment toward a person or place (whether due to a current situation or one from twenty years ago) it can be so overwhelming that in order to quiet the churning of resentment and anger they feel the need to self-medicate to turn off the noise.

For one's recovery to be strong and potential relapse to become a nonissue, there are several roads for the person in recovery to consider in dealing with resentment. Twelve Step meetings, sponsorship, counseling, and religious or spiritual engagement are all valid support systems to help a person in recovery to stay true to the desired course. Each of these options can also provide ample opportunities for venting resentments. If not resolved, resentments fester amidst the person's inner turmoil until they take the form of relapse or reckless actions.

When I was working as an evening treatment counselor in a rehabilitation recovery program, I heard my clients say all too often that they were resentful toward a partner, family member, or institution. They got into the mind set of, "I'll show them" or "They'll be sorry," and they went out and used or drank. Keep in mind that if people with addictions have transferred old resentments that were spawned from family members or friends years ago, and they have done nothing to deal with those resentments, then they might consequently place those resentments onto an unsuspecting and innocent victim with whom they are in a current relationship.

To you, the "normie" or "healthy one," resentments may cause a pimple or two, but usually our actions and emotions stay in check, we work through them, and we move on. The residual effect of resentment may produce some discomfort or even anger, but the outcome is rarely as detrimental as it can be for the alcoholic / addict.

The pity-pot to the alcoholic / addict is a handy way of keeping resentments alive. "Oh, woe is me, no one understands me; I was really dealt a bad hand, and nothing goes my way." Or they might think, "I'm doing the best I can, but I guess it's just not good enough." These are common monologues of self-pitying. People with addictions can find great comfort on their pity-pots, and if enough pity is allocated to them, then lo and behold, they have convinced themselves they have earned the right to drink or use. Anger fuels resentment, and resentment fuels anger. This is a vicious circle without an exit gate, and the alcoholic / addict may always find this as a strong reason to justify their relapse.

Alcoholic / addicts may tend to believe their own press that tells them they are no good or are failures. They may think that life has amounted to nothing and that they have accomplished little. Dreams and goals that they hoped for in younger days have taken a back seat due to addiction. Often they actually resent themselves more than others for allowing this to happen.

This resentment could be ongoing and perpetuate a steady buzz in the person's head; therefore, resentment presents fertile ground for relapse. Other than being open to communicating, there is nothing you can do as a family member or friend to help them deal with their resentment. Remember that some of that resentment might be about you for something you did or did not do—yesterday or even years earlier. It might be very hard for you to be impartial and difficult for your loved one to come forth with their issues, so it might not be a good idea to offer an empathetic ear.

I have had many clients report that their spouses, family members, or friends were growing more resentful toward them because they were striving and persevering in reaching their own personal goals as well as strengthening their boundaries and communication with their loved one.

Please don't allow the alcoholic / addict to clip your wings of growth, confidence, and dreams just because they are stuck on square one and, therefore, resent your determination to meet life's challenges head on. This can perpetuate the resentments that you both harbor toward each other. This does not make for an honest partnership or lend itself toward achieving the common goal of support that healthy partners should have for each other. When I was going through my divorce, I would tell my husband that until he got rid of his resentments toward me or old resentments that he had transferred to me, we would not have a chance for reconciliation.

His resentment toward me (as I pursued my dreams and goals) and his resentment toward himself (for not being able to pursue his dreams and goals) was the powder keg that I believe subconsciously blew us apart.

Boredom

As the statement goes: An idle mind is the devil's play ground. This is true for both the "healthy" individual and the alcoholic/addict, but boredom can be a major contributing factor in addiction and relapse.

Many people find themselves eating too much, gambling, shopping to excess, or indulging in other vices out of boredom. Therefore, routine and concrete scheduling can be a lifesaver for the alcoholic/addict. Knowing where to be and when to be there, as well as being accountable to someone or something else, provides a safe framework for the person who is new in recovery.

A lackluster disposition and attitude along with making plans to make plans can indicate that a person may have an issue with boredom. They might find themselves sluggish or having gotten used to putting off goals and dreams to another time, another day. It takes a lot of effort and persistence to shake the alcoholic/addict out of their comfort zone of boredom, for it has often been a big part of the person's lifestyle for many years.

Boredom is a state of mind. They may shut out the world by sleeping, vegging in front of the television or computer, or just hanging out listening to music. If they get bored of being bored, drugs or alcohol are an easy (not much effort required) place to go for relief. They need to snap themselves out of boredom, and this takes effort and commitment.

A schedule, coupled with passion for a new hobby or sporting activity, allows the alcoholic/addict to successfully and happily break the cycle of boredom. Though you don't want to have to cajole them out of boredom and then babysit your efforts, you can entertain some options toward a common hobby or event. Maybe plan a trip and enlist your loved one to aid you in these plans. If your loved one shows a propensity for classic cars or hot rods, buy an old one and refurbish it together. Direction, commitment, and interest could help fuel the alcoholic/addict away from this state of boredom.

Fear

Is the fear imagined or real? Is the fear based in reality (a head-on car collision) or rooted in the unknown? Whether an alcoholic/addict or not, most fear that anyone experiences is imagined. In fearing the unknown, we distrust an outcome and fear not being in control of what may or may not happen. The alcoholic/addict can be gripped by unknown or ungrounded fear, and this fear can cripple their ability to make important changes in life. For so long they have not been able to trust an outcome, and consequently they turned to drugs or alcohol to suppress their fear of … well, … fear. If fear is so crippling, then they may feel there is only one option—to relapse—instead of trusting their recovery program and what they have worked so hard to build and the spirituality of their higher power's guidance and protection.

Relapse can take on many shapes and forms. The important thing is not *what form* the relapse takes, or even *why* one relapses, but rather deciding *how* one will change and therefore commit to a stronger more formidable recovery program in the future. What can one learn from a misstep? Relapse doesn't have to be a hanging offense as you want to keep in mind all the previous clean and sober days.

The route of recovery can be a very circuitous path. Be mindful that at the end of the day, only the person recovering from addiction knows how strong their commitment to their recovery program is, and only they know whether they are practicing recovery or relapse.

Most of the shadows of this life are caused
by standing in one's own sunshine.

RALPH WALDO EMERSON

Chapter 19

SEVENTY-SEVEN (YES, I SAID 77) WARNING SIGNS OF RELAPSE

In the previous chapter we discussed the four major triggers to relapse. But relapse can rear its ugly head for a myriad of other excuses and reasons. The sun shining can be a damn good reason to drink, and a cloudy day is an understandable reason for some people to get high. Look under any rock or in any corner and there will be more reasons than one can list in a lifetime to justify a relapse. Ask the alcoholic/addict, for they can be very creative in their reasoning. If they want to relapse, they will, regardless of how many reasons they have or have not formulated to excuse the decision.

Here I offer a list of seventy-seven relapse warning signs. These symptoms are not listed in any particular order and are universal for the alcoholic and drug addict alike. If you observe your loved one with any of these symptoms over a period of time, it could be an indication that a relapse may be in the near future. No matter what they may say or do, please remember that you had NOTHING to do with the relapse. If the alcoholic/addict is "practicing" relapse instead of recovery, there isn't a single thing anyone, anywhere, can do about it. Their mind is already off and running with when and how relapse is going to take place.

My client Stacy was concerned that her husband was overreacting to stressful situations and those disappointments were more overwhelming than normal. He was working a clean and sober program for over a year and had strong support from his A.A. meetings as well as his sponsor. One day she reported that he had relapsed. When they discussed the relapse, she asked her husband why he had not called his sponsor. His answer was, "Because he would tell me not to do it." As almost comical as this sounds, the alcoholic / addict who is determined to relapse or practicing relapse instead of recovery has probably thought about it for a while, maybe even planned it out, and the last thing this person wants is to be talked out of it.

People planning to relapse are hell-bent on partnering up with their drug of choice, and though the ramifications do flow through their conscious thinking, their desires to use or drink again are just too great.

You can be on guard if you witness any of these symptoms, but remember that there is probably nothing you can do about their state of mind. If you feel inclined to bring up your concerns about what you are seeing, then fine, but please don't get your hopes up or have expectations that the outcome may be different than what the alcoholic / addict wants it to be; after all, they are in control of their recovery or lack of it.

This list was comprised over a number of years talking to hundreds of alcoholic / addicts.

1. Doubting their ability to stay sober
2. Denying their fears
3. Trying adamantly to convince themselves that they will never drink or use again
4. Deciding that being abstinent is "all I need"
5. Trying to force sobriety on others
6. Becoming overly confident about their recovery
7. Avoiding talking about their problems and their recovery
8. Behaving compulsively (overworking, underworking, overtalking)
9. Expressing that things fall short of what they want
10. Expressing that things fall short of what they think they deserve
11. Finding disappointments more overwhelming than normal
12. Being very impatient in dealing with everyday living
13. Changing locale when bored or frustrated with the current one
14. Nebulous, uncertain, disjointed, or unrealistic future plans
15. Overreacting to stressful situations
16. Isolating themselves
17. Becoming preoccupied with one area of their life
18. Experiencing depression
19. Planning haphazardly

20. Setting unrealistic schedules
21. Living in the past
22. Daydreaming and indulging in wishful thinking
23. Viewing problems as unsolvable
24. Longing for happiness, but not knowing how to define it
25. Avoiding having fun
26. Believing "I'm no good, nobody likes me"
27. Analyzing excessively
28. Becoming irrational with friends and family
29. Experiencing periods of confusion
30. Becoming easily angered
31. Blaming people, places, and things for their problems
32. Doubting the disease
33. Believing that "their way" of recovery is preferable to a Twelve Step program or therapy
34. Eating irregularly
35. Becoming listless for extended periods of time
36. Sleeping irregularly (a great deal or very little)
37. Losing their daily routine
38. Attending Twelve Step meetings sporadically
39. Making excuses for sporadic attendance to Twelve Step meetings
40. Failing to call their sponsor
41. Developing an "I don't care attitude"
42. Developing a "poor me" attitude
43. Stating with agitation that others "don't understand what I'm going through"
44. Adopting an increasingly defensive posture
45. Rejecting help openly
46. Developing imaginary aches and pains
47. Acting increasingly unreliable
48. Becoming unable to establish or keep eye contact in conversation
49. Becoming too comfortable or complacent in recovery
50. Showing a demeanor of profound or ongoing boredom
51. Indicating a fear of success
52. Rationalizing that drinking/using can't make their life worse than it already is
53. Feeling powerless and helpless
54. Developing fantasies about social drinking/using again

55. Beginning to lie consciously with no remorse for doing so
56. Taking nonprescription medication regularly
57. Losing all confidence in themselves
58. Having trouble performing simple tasks
59. Making major life changes
60. Experiencing life changes
61. Developing unreasonable resentments
62. Feeling overwhelmed with loneliness
63. Feeling overwhelmed with frustration and anger
64. Feeling overwhelming tension
65. Visiting drinking "buddies"
66. Visiting drinking places
67. Acting overzealous about things
68. Losing interest too quickly in projects or opportunities
69. Losing focus at work
70. Losing commitment toward work
71. Convincing themselves, "I'm cured"
72. Rationalizing that it's okay to partake if it's not their drug of choice
73. Pointing out everyone else's flaws and problems
74. Becoming increasingly antisocial
75. Changing their mind all the time
76. Doubting their decisions constantly
77. Finding difficulty experiencing the simple pleasures of life

As I noted previously, there is really nothing you can do if your loved one is hell-bent on relapsing; However, you don't have to sit idly by if that's just not your nature. With that said, what can you do if you see or sense these symptoms? Your actions, or lack thereof, should depend upon the relationship you have. If your loved one has relapsed time and time again, you may be too weary to deal with it once again. On the other hand, there is nothing wrong in saying, "I've noticed that you seem more despondent lately," "I've noticed you've been hanging out with the old gang," or "I can't help but be concerned that you might be jeopardizing your sobriety. I'm here for you if you want to talk." These are caring and genuine statements that still allow you to stay neutral and not engage. You are stating your concern and discomfort with what you are seeing. Just be prepared that the alcoholic/addict may respond with, "There's nothing wrong; no need to worry." It is unlikely that you will hear, "Hey, you're right; thanks for pointing it out. I'll get to a meeting right away."

Conversely, don't waste your breath and adopt an anxious nature that says, "Oh, my God, you're sleeping more than normal" or "You aren't going to your meetings," and then asking, "Are you going to relapse or have you already relapsed?" These comments open the door for engagement and surely don't keep you neutral. Be wary of automatically accepting whatever response you get back, as it may not be the truth. The person in addiction recovery often retains some of the duplicitous tendencies of this disease for some time, and they may lie about symptoms they know might indicate a potential relapse.

If relapse becomes a reality, know that you have a strong recovery plan or contract in place between you and your loved one, and you will be armed and ready to implement those previously discussed consequences or ramifications.

Better keep yourself clean and bright;
you are the window through which you must see the world.
GEORGE BERNARD SHAW

Section Five

ESSAYS AND POEMS FROM THE WORLD OF ADDICTION AND RECOVERY

For years, I worked as a counselor at The Salvation Army Adult Rehabilitation Center and the Council on Alcoholism and Drug Abuse in Santa Barbara, California. Working with clients in both individual and group therapy, we explored a myriad of topics about recovery and relapse, as well as emotional and cognitive ups and downs.

In order to keep things interesting, I sometimes asked my clients to write a "Dear John" letter to their drug of choice. I have kept a number of them, and with their permission and first name only in authorship, I have incorporated some of them in this book. In addition, they have contributed some poems and essays that they found pertinent and interesting.

I cared very deeply for these men and women. I grew to respect and admire their strength and dignity, but at the same time I sometimes wanted to slap them for the poor decisions and choices they had made or continued to make in their lives. I did not keep up with their lives once they graduated from the program, but my daily prayers always include them.

Why have I included them in this book? I wanted you to see what can go on in the heads of people addicted to alcohol or drugs who may wish to truly and genuinely shed themselves of their disease. These essays, poems, and letters have not been altered in anyway—misspellings, grammar errors, and all remain. Please be aware that some of these may be emotionally difficult to read.

Chapter 20

WORDS FROM
THE ALCOHOLIC/ADDICT

Dear Booze,

I can still remember our first date on that warm summer night in 1976. Even though I only got to first base that night, you made my senses tingle, and introduced me feelings I didn't know existed. The fact that our relationship was forbidden only made it more exciting for me. Back then, we didn't get to be together often, usually just on the weekends, but when we were, you made me feel so light headed and sure of myself.

I was so grateful that we were able to stay together when I moved away to college. After a long day of classes, studying, and work, it was wonderful to be able to unwind with you in the evenings. And on the weekends, we could really get quality time together, walking hand in hand through the streets of Isla Vista.

In the years between college and kids, our relationship got a little out of hand. Sometimes I enjoyed your company to excess. Our little ménage-a-trios with Blackjack got us into some big trouble. We could hang out for 24 hours straight sometimes. I'll never forget when the South Lake Tahoe sheriff decided to split us up, and I fought them until they had turned me black and blue with their Billy clubs, and locked me up so I couldn't see you.

I was glad when we decided I should have a life outside of you, but that we would reserve time everyday just for ourselves, on one else. If felt fun and forbidden, like the old days.

But little by little, you wanted more and more of me for yourself. And

I have come to realize that while I still love you, in fact crave you, that our relationship is unhealthy, and I have to end it forever if I want to be happy.

Don't take it too bad. It's not you, it's me. I'm sure you will make someone else out there very happy.

Dave

Hello my love, Heroin, friend for so long. I grew up just watching and yearning to be part of your life. My whole family loved you and you helped make them successful. I loved what they had, what you gave them, new cars, beautiful women, nice cloths, jewelry, and respect from all walks of life. I grew up wanting to meet you. When I became of age, I met you. The first go around with you, you let three of us taste you for about a week. Then I got scared because without you I got sick. So I stayed away from you for a few years, but I knew, really knew that I missed you. The first time I ran away from you, all I did was think of you. I even had some fun with your cousin Coca (Cocaine). But it was nothing like you, so of course, I brought you back to my arms and loved you more then life its self. You were the only love I knew for too many years. I wanted to leave you but I just couldn't leave or be without you. Our relationship became a love hate situation. I loved it when you were good, even more when you became weight, cause that just meant money. You were smart and knew that I liked money. So you made sure you kept it with me. Some people called me a junkie because we were together, and at times I wondered about our relationship. But, you kept me in business. You sent me to places that were just in people's dreams, from Beverly Hills to Skid Row in Downtown Los Angeles. You always kept me a businessman just for you. You taught me how to joke around, to act a fool, how to dance and smile, and to dream. I just liked and hated the way you made me burn my shirts, my pants and fingers. In a funny way that's when I liked you the best. When you changed your name to Baluchi, man oh man, I thought you were the best. Around that time, I met my first wife. She was cool but she liked money and not you. I let her go and kept you instead. Then I got this girl pregnant and I just thought, FUCK, and you just said Fuck it. I truly wanted to do the right thing, so I married the mother of my kids and let her know of you. She didn't mind you at first, and of course, all I did was think of you. Three kids later once again I chose you over them. I got tired of doing time for you, so I met another friend called Recovery. Soon after, met another that I called friend that even you could not destroy. You see, when I met recovery I found your controlling ways were not love. You were just empty dreams and loneliness. I didn't know that I was so alone, you would just cover it up. I didn't know what cold bone was till you were gone. With my friend Recovery I found myself and that I possessed a mind, body and soul with a heart of warmth and care. You taught me to forget when I needed to remember. Well now I say, see-ya, much, later. I'm cool without you and all your bullshit situations you got me into. I found a friend first in me, but you came back and took my friend Recovery for a while. But you fucked up when I met another person and myself who believed in me. Even you couldn't take me from her. You lost your power today and I pray I have a lot more today's, one day at a time, without you. So one day at a time…bye, bye, bye!

Later,
Albert

Recovery

Going through this previous experience of relapse I have learned a lot more about myself. Being incarcerated and being surrounded by criminals has slapped me into knowing what I do not want to be. I do not want to put myself in jeopardy of losing my family, friends, and education. I wouldn't want to end up in life knowing that I lost the most important things to me over stupid decisions. I have a lot of ambition in life to make it somewhere, the worst feeling in life is knowing you threw that all away yourself while making decisions with a mind not yet taken over with maturity.

The biggest thing I received from this experience was learning a sense of maturity. I believe the main reason I made bad decisions was due to the fact that I had yet to be forced to make better decisions thinking of the long run outcome. Most young people have a point when they become forced to mature. Otherwise we just keep thinking on the whim rather than remember how it will affect us in the long run. When making the bad decisions I chose to, I was not thinking about the negative aspects of what could happen. In other words I was being selfish just thinking about what would satisfy me at the moment. Being put in jail was a huge slap in the face. All of a sudden I was forced to realize how I affected others and myself by my bad decisions. I can try to blame it on someone else, but I have definitely learned its time to take fault for my decisions.

My family and friends became very disappointed in me when learning about my incarceration previously, and I only let them down more by relapsing. I am most grateful that the ones closest to me understand that people aren't perfect and we all make mistakes. By making mistakes we only learn. In recovery there is a grate motivation to not relapse, but we all know there is still room for mistakes. In my case my relapse became my eye opener, a reassurance of what I do not want to be. Being put in jail over a weakness is such a disappointing feeling to myself. I have let myself down most of all. Just proving to myself that I am better than the people I was locked up with is enough motivation to get my act together. What I saw was the exact opposite of who I want to be. Being compared to these people only by my bad decisions makes me realize how weakness ruins people's lives and I never saw myself as weak, but have proven wrong by being forced to reflect on the negative in my life. I no longer will allow the weakness to subside in my life. I have gained an inner confidence and motivation to better myself. I have a father that chose to let his weakness take over his life and caused him to lose everything he had that ever meant anything. I have made bad decisions like my father, but I will not turn out the way he did. I am better than that; sometimes people become more aware from experience I know I am one of them.

I vow to make my life the best it can be and to not hinder my opportunity to make something of myself by making immature decisions. I have learned to think about the outcome of my decisions in the long run and how they will affect the people closest to me and most importantly myself. I plan on moving to help get rid of the high pressure that exists where I live and the constant opportunities that present themselves that would further negatively affect my future. I am going to finish the school year and proceed on working hard and keeping in mind my main goals in life. I will no longer let my weaknesses decide my future. I thank Prop 36 and everyone in the program that has made me a stronger person and supported me through my times. Thank you for the guidance and more importantly the realization that my future is worth something fighting for.

Anthony

My drug of choice is Mary Jane:

I love you Mary Jane. You make me fill so good you would make me fill no pane. Mary Jane made my day everyday not worrying not careing about people looking at me not careing about what I eat and she wouldn't let me worry about my problems she would say they would all go away. I started smokeing her when I was 11 years old and she was the best thing I had ever had in my life. I loved her very much. Everytime I had her she would give me this Natural High that I loved and it was going for a couple of years and every bit was worth it but one day it would catch up to me and it did. By putting me in jail and programs ever seen's I was a little kid I didn't lisen so I keep going intel I was a man and then it hit me and it hit me hard and that's when I opened my eyes really big and said it's time for me to stop! Because she was putting my family aside and friend's but she stop't when I said that's all I can't go know further because she wasn't taking me no wear. I've been clean and sober from her for about 8 months and I fill very good and I have my head on straight and thinking straight too it's the best thing I've had in my life and I am going to keep it this way because family and friends are their and care for me and been by my side every bit of the way. So I would like to say to her is good bye and I will never see you again.

From Frank

Let's see…My God, where do I begin? I am a 34 year old, white female, from Santa Barbara, CA. And I also happen to be what they sometimes call a "hope to die dope fiend." In my 34 years on this planet and I have probably been thorough more heartache and pain, and just BAD, BAD luck, then most people will experience in their whole life time. My parents divorced when I was 12 years old, my mom just came and picked up my brother and I from school one day, and said, "Guess what guys? We have a new house to go home to today." At first we were both very happy because, my parents were two people who should have never been together. They fought constantly, barely spoke a word to each other, they would actually fist fight in front of my brother and I as children. So, she picked us up from school, and put a restraining order on my father. All I remember is being really confused , and haunted by the thought of what my father must have went through that day when he came home form work, and his whole life was just gone.

   Shortly after that, I began acting out by shoplifting. I would ditch school with my friends, and we would just go stealing. Stealing anything and everything we wanted, clothes mostly. And it was such a rush, the feeling of getting away with that. As a minor, I did get caught twice for that, once at the Broadway, and once at Nordstrom. But since we were minors, we got a slap on the wrist, and a fine. I do remember the second time in court being labeled a "juvenile delinquent" by the judge, and I just rolled my eyes at him. I did not care. At 15 my mother kicked me out for telling her to shut-up. Wait, let me go back a bit, as a child my mother was EX-TREMELY strict. We were not allowed to play with the other kids in the neighborhood because they weren't good enough, or they were "dirty" So, I remember as a child, my brother and I just sitting in the window, watching the kids play outside, and we weren't allowed. Basically my brother was all I really had. She also had a very short fuse. Everything we did irritated her, and everything we said she didn't believe. So, she kicked me out at 15, and I went back with my dad, and my little brother. Now, my dad worked 10 hour days at the hospital, so my brother and I had run of the house. I never went to school, I always ditched and my friends and I we would come back here and drink beer, and smoke pot, blast music real loud, raid my dad's room, to see what we could find. One time I found a bag of insulin syringes hidden in his vent, along with what my friend said was Cocaine.

   I had a hard time in school, I started having sex with these boys from the wrongest crowd I could've possibly gone with. I would have sex with one of them, and then the next day at school, they would yell and abuse me, call me a whore, etc. etc. After high school, I moved to Hawaii for 4 mo's to help my cousin out with her kid, and while there, I did alot of thinking, and alot of realizing what a naive dummy I had been. I became so disgusted with myself, and the things that I had allowed people to do to me, that I couldn't even look at myself in the mirror without crying. Almost immediately after I got home, my friend came over with some speed, and i jumped on it without giving it a thought. The thought was more like

"FINALLY" Because I had never come across hard drugs until that point. I had just been doing pot, acid, ecstasy, and alcohol. So, I started snorting speed, and that lasted for about 2 years. I left my dad's house, by choice, to couch surf with my friend, and just do drugs. That friend had left me one night for some guy, left me alone to fend for myself, cuz we kinda looked out for each other, or so I thought. Anyway, I ended up hooking up with this older lady, who had just gotten out of prison, and who was also a prostitute, and a heroin addict. One night, she offered me some and I said no at first, because i had never used needles before, and then it took me about 7 minutes to change my mind. She shot me up for my first time, and I never stopped. I puked my guts out all night, and loved it anyway. It was like I had finally found what I had been looking for. I boosted from stores, and then returned the stolen items to support my habit. I stole from my jobs, I even stole from my dad, the ONLY person who stood by me and loved me anyway. So, anyway, long story longer...:) Heroin gave me so much. Let's see...countless friends dead and gone, the love and trust of my father, 4 trips to the State Penitentiary, countless trips to county jail. One of my boyfriends was then shot and killed while I was in prison, over Heroin of course.

Then I met another guy just like me. This one was without a doubt the love of my life. We ended up having a child together. A gorgeous baby boy, who is now 2 1/2 years old, and the Real love of my life. The last time I went to jail, I found out I was pregnant the night I arrived, and got out of the penitentiary when I was about 7 mo's pregnant. I was 32 at that time, I was ecstatic, I felt like this baby was what I had been waiting for for years, and I also happened to be in love with his dad, I just thought that everything was gonna be ok now. The 7 mo's I was incarcerated, I didn't even take any cold medication, not even ONE drag off a cigarette. nothing! And I was very sure of myself that I would not use when I got home. And then I got home. My son's father was acting distant, and I thought it was because I was big and fat, and it was something about this town, that was all I had ever done here, was use. Everyone, including doctor's were telling me that heroin wasn't so bad for baby, it was the crack and meth that was terrible. And I did it. I used while I was 7 months pregnant. Something I thought I'd never do. So, heroin had already taken my whole life from me already, years of freedom, it also took my son's father from me, who unfortunately overdosed on Jan. 30th, 2009. And now I was facing the ultimate sacrifice.

Losing my child. Luckily that didn't happen, and I would not be where I am today if it was not for him. Lord knows I aint perfect, I slipped once or twice, but I have remained un-addicted for over two years now, I have held down the same job for two years now, where I even received a promotion. I actually see my father as a friend now, the most important person in my life, the one that never turned his back on me no matter what, and most importantly my son who is the absolute love of my life, and brings me unexplainable joy every day. My father told me once that drugs are for cowards who can't deal with reality, people who have no back bone, and can't just stand up and face whatever comes their way. And I will never forget that, for he is so right. Jail or a coffin, those are the only places drugs will ever lead you. You may get away with it for a week, a year, or 10 years even, but eventually, it will ruin you. That's a promise and a guarantee.

Hollie

Miss Cocaine

Why I loved being with you. While I was with you, you made feel like a flying bird. You made me feel good when I was angry, sad, stressed and even happy. You were introduced to me by friends and family. I first knew you as powder. It was nice having you around at parties or even hanging out with friends. That lasted about two or three good years. I then met you as rock cocaine. Then you became my priority. I didn't want to be around anyone when I was with you, all my attention was on you. I became less social and kept everything inside. You made me feel so good I didn't want to be around anyone anymore. I put everything and everyone behind me. I hurt a lot of people especially myself because of you. Even though I don't regret meeting you I have to let you go. I had lots of good times. But the more I got closer the worse my life got. This is why I'm saying bye.

Lou

Dear Meth.

Respectfully. I will start with a brief background statement: addiction can be an asset as easily as one's worst enemy: it can provide focus on a multi-faceted view of the world, as well as delimiting one's path to the confines of a fixed circle, like on a tread-wheel, never able to find new ground. We have the choice: to be Time's prisoner on a ferris wheel ride (that's you) that was new and unlike any others I had experienced—it was surrounded with water and acted like a tread mill. Of course, the advertisement bling for this ride completely blocked the cautionary signs, and of course, being the tried and true candidate for trying anything new, good or bad, I stepped aboard. Your ride was instantly the most fun and energizing ride I had ever been on. What I didn't realize was the longevity of this sea-bearing launch until I recently exited.

I enjoyed the ride so thoroughly that I eventually forgot all about my responsibilities and purpose. I lost track of what I valued and where I was going professionally. But I faked the increasing pain and misguidance I was creating, thinking that as long as I could continue enjoying the ride and kept my money in my pocket, everything would be fine. But the attendee kept asking for more money every other time the dipped in the water, so I kept delving it out, as long as I could maintain the fun and be aware of my budget…And by the time there was no longer a budget, I realized what a rip-off it was, and only to maintain some artificial feeling. Ah, and what a relief it was to finally step off board this ride..it was like I had been trapped in a time machine ; when I stepped off the ride, I had only grown older, but everything was the same, if not worse from neglect.

I must acknowledge how well your scheme works, taking people's money for the promise of a rouse, a good time that, as long as the pay, will be indefinite. Once they exit, they'll only see the sadness of all they neglected…yet another reason to lure them back on, in hopes that they'll continue to deny themselves a respite; a chance to not look at their lives spinning out of control.

Cordially,
Passenger no longer

Say Goodbye?

I do not feel capable at this time of saying good-bye to my lover, my best friend, my way of life for the past 28 years. However, I offer you this:

Why I Love You So Much

My mind is thoroughly engaged and engrossed with you always.

Thoughts of your cunningness, taste, effect and affect, powerfulness, feeling, and above all else; the manner in which you make me feel about myself, always intrigue me. And what is there to say about our intimacy? The most wonderful attribute about our relationship is the intricate intimacy. The essence, the innermost, the personal, the private, the familiarity, the informality that is always there when we are together.

To sit at the bar and know each other so well. To sit at the bar and see you, touch you, whisper to you, know you, and feel the intimacy that will always be between us. There is no other who can make me feel as you do. The martini glass is just a vessel, the olives mere dressing; however the power is in you; the gin. How comfortable you make me feel. The confidence you instill in me. All things seem possible after ingesting you three or four or more times in one sitting. You are capable of utter transformation. Cold, frosty green bottles full of a different and distinct aroma fill my mouth, taste buds and tummy in the form of beer. I imagine the splendor of the people who gather around us, my increased confidence in myself, the more esteem that pours forth out of you, and on such a pedestal I sit when you are with me and inside of me. To relax with you at home or in the bar, in the part or at the beach or in the car; and especially, at social gatherings of prime significance, you are always there for me. Companionship that reaches new highs and levels. I enjoy so much more around me when you are intimately at my side. The conversation grows with anticipation, healthy debates are more scholarly, comedy and laughter seem richer…good times…good times. And the intelligence, attractiveness and all else come so much easier through our blessed union. You make me feel so powerful. Again, you make me feel so powerful. And this adds pleasure, happiness and joy to my life. To finish working and have you as a cold six-pack sitting next

to me in the car on the way home…not even drinking you, ingesting you, just the knowledge you are with me. The enchanting mornings we spend together on days off work are filled with bliss.

Ohh, how I love you. And you are always there…and I know the craving is mutual. I cannot fathom life without you. However, I cannot fathom life with you…

Why I despise you so much:

My mind is thoroughly engaged and engrossed with you always. Your omnipresence is overwhelming and everlasting. With you I am not permitted to sleep properly, eat, feel, cry or laugh. You are such a jealous lover and take no prisoners; you want all my attention and there is no time for any other person or engagement. I despise our jealous and dominate consumption of my life. My obsession of you has caused me to lose all others in my life. When I say enough of you, you say "no more of me".

Conclusion of this matter:

The end is near for both of us. Our relationship has matured. It was once fun, but has grown incessant and unsatisfying. As much as I love you, I must admit separation forever is the only conclusion I can reach. Without you, many people, places and things will be afforded the opportunity to return to my life. I will accept them with a grateful smile and humble heart. You, however, may not return. You must stay away and this is so difficult for us both. Tonight I say: "Good bye martinis, Molson ice, B&B and all other forms of alcohol. Good bye!

Mike

To my dearest Crystal,

Hey baby, whats up? Nothing really new with me since I parted ways with you. Its hard to let you go because we have had SO many good times with each other since I was 15 years old. We hopefully should not see each other again because we always end up in trouble, lots of trouble. I wish I could say that we will never see each other again, but my experience with you in the past, I have made the same vows but time and time again those vows were always broken. You have been no good to me since I was 18. You have sent me to jails and countless institutions time after time. My life has never amounted to anything because of you. People think of me as unreliable and not trustworthy because of the way that you would make me find you. Even though we are not together anymore, I still have to deal with many repercussions of the actions that I have done while I was under your influence. You have made me a worthless piece of society. I have become a complete loser with a near hopeless future. Everyday I have to deal with miserable people that shout orders at me if I don't follow their so-called "suggestions". All this I get to deal with thanks to you. There was once a time when everything was alright. But that was many years ago. It makes me wonder if there will ever be a day where I have escaped your grasp. But deep down I know that you'll always be waiting for me. And maybe this time will be different and hopefully I will be able to find ways to help me keep away from you. But until then I will just have to be content with my programs. Either though people talk about you all the time I will have to concentrate on all the bad times we've had because those times outweigh the good times by far. So goodbye Crystal.

Your friend,
Joe

Take An Alcoholic's Word For It
By Anonymous

Don't allow me to lie to you and accept it for the truth—in so doing, you encourage me to lie. The truth may be painful but get at it.

Don't let me outsmart you. This only teaches me to avoid responsibility and to lose respect for you at the same time.

Don't let me exploit you or take advantage of you. In so doing, you become an accomplice to my evasion of responsibility.

Don't lecture me, moralize, scold, praise, blame or argue when I'm drunk or sober. And don't pour out my liquor. You may feel better but the situation will be worse.

Don't accept my promises. This is just my method of postponing pain. And don't keep switching agreements. If an agreement is made, stick to it.

Don't lose your temper with me. It will destroy you and any possibility of helping me.

Don't allow your anxiety for us to compel you to do what I must do for myself.

Don't cover up or abort the consequences of my drinking. It reduces the crisis but perpetuates the illness.

Above all, don't run away from reality as I do. Alcoholism, my illness, gets worse as my use continues. Start now to learn to understand…

("Open Letter to My Family," written by an alcoholic, distributed by The Sequoia Center, and published in *If You Loved Me, You'd Stop!* by Lisa Frederiksen.)

Heroin when we first met you made me feel like I never felt before. You gave me so much energy and joy you made me bounce with happienes and made me for get all my problems. It was like all my problems went away. I was abel to make long love with my ladie and worrie free. Then when you wernt around it would make me sick with worrie. I did not want to get up out of bed are do anything. I just had to have you all the time. But then I realized that all you really did was get me in trouble and you were the reason I was getting sick. My troubles were not going away at all they were still there but my family was not. I know I have to stay away from you are you will be the death of me. So I have to say good by to you for ever.

Joseph

Goodbye to Cocaine

You've been a friend, or at least I thought so for many years. You carried me through the pain of a very sick marriage and all the years of depression. I considered you a close, intimate friend. Almost like a lover. That's why I've called you my lady in white. But like a lady, a lover, you reduced me; blinded me until I was trapped in your warm embrace. You took me from a good man, a good husband and father to the degrigation and humility of the courts, jails and total self disgust. Everything I am and everything I had I gave to you and like a lover you spit it back at me. Took me to my knees. No more. I will no longer bow to your soft voice disguised as a sweet song, when in reality it is a song of death or self destruction. You've blinded me, broken my heart for the last time. I still think of you often like I would with a long time lover who had wounded me deeply. Goodbye my old friend, my old enemy.

Never again will I taste your kisses, as much as I may at times still want to. You are not taking me down again. You will not cause my death or incarceration ever again.

Good bye forever to my Lady in White.

Tony

Dear Alcohol,

I am writing to you for a specific purpose. That purpose is dump your sleesy,easy, ass and to make you see that we weren't meant to be. I'm sorry but there can no longer be the two of us. From now on there's me, and then there's you. I cannot continue this relationship we have going on. I repeat, I cannot continue this relationship we have going on. Since I met you, you have done nothing but given me problems. I can't keep my head straight with anything I do because you confuse me and make me stumble on my path of life. I am so over being a part of this dysfunction. Over the past few years of our lives together, we had fun but that fun usually resulted in someone getting hurt; of course you never suffered from it because I know someone else would have their lips on you after I left. I know you don't care about me and that's why I don't care about you. You changed me. My family always told me to leave you but I didn't listen. The few people that loved me warned me about you. My friends didn't really care because they were having fun with their lips on you too. I was never the type to share my lover, well…At least not you. Do you remember when we yearned for each others company, my mouth on your body. Our love affair had me abused for my money and my mind. If only we would have had a healthier relationship maybe we wouldn't be in this position. Look girl what I'm trying to say is that we need our space to grow and figure out what we want. I know what you want, you just want the next person to fall for your traps but that won't be me. Nope, you played me for too long. I am not a lollypop and don't like be played for a sucker. In other words take your beautiful labeled clothes and your beautiful shape and find the next buster to control. I control my own destiny and will not let you or another person take that from me anymore. I can't even thank you for the times we had because they were never good memories or weren't memories at all. You are not worth it because you take me away from my real purpose in life. I know that my purpose is not to make a life with you. I have a new love in my life and don't need this, I have many things to worry about like my family, my piece of mind, my education, my job, my money, my health, and apparently my clean and sober group now. Can't forget that carrot head probation officer. I just have no room for you at this point and would appreciate it if you didn't come back into my life with temptations. I knew you would understand.

Your ex-friend,
Manuel

I Am Meth

I destroy homes, I tear families apart; I take children, that's just a start.

I'm more costly than diamonds, more precious than gold, the sorrow I bring is a sight to behold.

If you need me, remember I'm easily found; I live all around you—in schools, and in towns.

I live with the rich, I live with the poor, I live down the street, and maybe next door.

I'm made in a lab, but not like you think; I can be made under your kitchen sink;

In your child's closet, and even in the woods; if this scares you to death, well it certainly should.

I have many names, but there's one you know best-I'm sure you've heard of me, my name's Crystal Meth

My power is awesome, try me, you'll see—but if you do you'll never break free.

Just try me once, I might let you go, but try me twice and I'll own your soul.

When I possess you, you'll steal and you'll lie. You do what you have to, just to get high.

The crimes you commit for my narcotic charms will be worth the pleasure you'll feel in your arms.

You'll lie to your mother, you'll steal from your dad; when you see their tears, and you might feel sad.

But you'll forget your morals and how you were raised; I'll be your conscience, I'll teach you my ways.

I take kids from parents, parents from kids; I turn people from God and separate friends.

I'll take everything from you—your looks and your pride; I'll be with you always, right by your side.

You'll give up everything—down to the bone; and then realize you're surely alone.

I'll take and take till you have nothing more to give; when I'm finally done with you, you'll be lucky to live.

If you try me, be warned, this is no game—if given the chance, I'll drive you insane.

I'll ravish your body; I'll control your mind. I'll own you completely;

your soul will be mine.

The nightmares I'll give you while you're lying in bed, the voices you'll hear from inside your head.

The sweats; the shakes, the visions you'll see—I want you to know these are all gifts from me.

But then it's too late, and you know in your heart that you will always be mine and we'll never part.

You'll regret that you tired me; they always do, but you came to me, not I to you.

You knew this would happen, many times you were told, but you challenged my power and chose to be bold.

You could have said no and just walked away; if you could live that day over, now what would you say?

I'll be your master, you'll be my slave; I'll even go with you when you go to your grave.

Now that you have met me, what will you do? Will you try me or not…it's all up to you.

I can bring you more misery than words can tell; come take my hand, let me lead you to hell.

Anonymous

When it gets dark enough, you can see the stars.

CHARLES A. BEARD

Chapter 21

WORDS FROM FAMILY MEMBERS AND FRIENDS

Like the previous chapter, this one is an offering of essays and tender reflections written by family members and friends about their loved ones' addiction.

As the counselor of these caring, loving people, I am grateful that they have opened their soul and heart to share their experiences, strength, and hope with me and you. These essays are here to show you that you are not alone, and that wherever you live, whatever your religious affiliation, financial status, sexual preference, age, creed, or color, addiction knows no boundaries. A heart is a heart, and it breaks when our loved ones are in trouble.

My son, an only child, is now 24 years old and has had a drug addiction for almost ten years. A trying ten years, to be sure. Yet, one moment stands out:

One dark morning in March 2001 two burly strangers came to our house, woke our innocent child up and, as planned, accompanied him to a Wilderness program in Idaho, and then, three weeks later, to a stark rehabilitation program in rural Utah. He was so young and innocent then; this was one of my darkest hours.

Just six months earlier optimism reigned. Our son had graduated from an excellent private middle school and began high school with the greatest expectations. He was playing on the freshmen football team, taking some advance placement courses, and was extraordinarily popular with girls and boys alike. Yet only a few weeks into his freshman year things quickly began to unravel. From over the counter drugs, to prescription drugs, to marijuana, to cocaine, to mushrooms and to L.S.D. Heroin would come a short time later. By the time he was spirited away to his first rehab program but six months later he had been enrolled in four different high schools.

During the next nine years he has had but brief periods of sobriety, having unsuccessfully been through innumerable inpatient and outpatient rehab programs and has served multiple incarcerations for drug related offences. Then, ten months ago, he was served two federal indictments for heroin related offences, and now sits in federal prison serving a five year sentence.

But the father-son story is not that simple nor does it end there. Indeed, this difficult and disappointing decade has been transformative to me, his father, in a very positive sense.

Ten years later I am a far better person than I was at the outset of my son's disease and the father-son relationship is more meaningful and profound than fathers typically have with their twenty something offspring. I attribute this growth to two things: my experience as an active Al-Anon member and the highly personal connections I have made with others living with the same challenge.

This is what I have learned and what has not only sustained me but enriched me:

1. I am not alone. There are so many out there that have dealt with a similar or even more uncomfortable scenario. In many cases my "partners" are fellow Al Anon members; in other instances they are friends or professional colleagues that shared that they too had a close family member struggling with addiction. In both instances, I have found that there is strength in numbers and that people are overwhelmingly kind of heart.

2. You help yourself by helping others. Five years into my Al-Anon experience I have helped innumerable others to deal with similar challenges to my own. Such "giving" has been cathartic to me and has helped put my son's addiction in perspective. I have become

a staunch advocate of the adage "it is far better to give than to receive."

3. Spirituality is a blessing. Although I feel that the latent spark of spirituality has always been part of my being, I never considered myself spiritual. Yet the saying "nobody is an atheist in a foxhole" is so true. I have been comforted to learn when and how to turn things over to higher power.

4. Everything happens for a reason. I sort of, kind of, believed this adage ten years ago; now I consider it an absolute truth. I doubt that my son would have survived if he had not been incarcerated; now, ten months into his incarceration, an incredible, beautiful person seems to be emerging. Likewise, our extraordinary father-son relationship would not have developed if it had not been for these years. The personal depth that I have acquired also would not have happened. Never underestimate the opportunities for growth that can emerge from the ashes of tragedy.

As our son sits in a federal prison cell 200 miles from his home I am filled with optimism and hope. We speak almost daily, visit often and have exchanged scores of meaningful letters. He has been sober since he entered prison ten months ago and is focused on his nutrition, working out, and attaining as many college level credits as possible. We both recognize that addiction is a disease that must be addressed one day at a time. And we realize that our son will have to address his disease every day for the rest of his life.

Yet, I proceed knowing that as long as we are both breathing the air of our fair earth, I will remain optimistic and focused on the unanticipated good, rather than the bad, that has come out of my son's battle with drug addiction.

Frank L.

We are best when we are gliding. We move across the smooth, slick floor in unison as if we were the only two people in the large room. We each know our job and we are careful to stay within the invisible edges of each other's peripheral views. The crowd is cheering, I know this because I can see them more than anything, and feel the vibration—but I cannot hear individual voices. We are in our tunnel, on our court, and the game is ours. My arm is long—outstretched to his as he reaches toward me—muscles glinting with sweat. I take the ball. I am strong; my mind is clear and focused. I can see better this way—when we are a team moving together up and down the court.

Then I pause. The ceiling parts above. I can see dark clouds in the East as they move toward us overhead. I look to him and he is unaware. The court has moved outside where it's dark and cold. The clouds overtake him and he is stopped in the center-shielded from me. It smells like new rain—but not fresh—just damp and musty on hot gravel. I cannot penetrate this shroud. There is a small streetlight shining in the distance illuminating one side of him frozen on the court. The darkness buries him deeper and deeper. The crowd has disappeared. The other players are blurred and then gone as I focus on him and try to pull him out with my mind. This has happened before and I have waited for the darkness to pass. This time, I lack the patience.

He is my father, 10 years passed. But I cannot address this similarity, as I have long forgiven his trespasses—as was expected of me. He is now my husband and, though I know he should stand accountable for his own actions, he carries the burden of many years of mistrust. Nightly, he sits in the same green armchair, sipping the same amber drink, watching the same mind numbing television. And so I don't trust myself for hating to see this—because sometimes I wonder who it is I'm hating. I don't trust the warning signs that scream out at me to leave, to not commit to this life. But I do so badly want to trust him, as he asks me to do—to let go of all of the others before him—to see him for who he "truly" is. Who is that? Will I like him if I really see him? Is it easier to vilify him as some alcoholic beast so that I can get my way, draw the line of our differences and move on again to another relationship...one that will be "perfect this time". Then I'll have to really look at myself and I will be alone with no one to lean on and no one to shine against. What's wrong with me? I should just appreciate these wonderful gifts that I have...these amazing similarities we do have instead of always trying to highlight our differences. I should just try to relax and allow us to work together instead of stepping back and reacting to the agitation I feel at the conflict and stress which swirl around our very different personalities.

And now there's someone else to consider. And any good parent would tell you she's the one that requires the protection anyway. She will see him later and I will not. She will be the bigger person who loves him and talks about him and what a loving, kind, fun person he is. And I will be the lonely, too-particular work-a-holic left at home, having thrown our family away because he never picked up after himself, because some mornings he left the house like the absent minded professor with his pant leg tucked into his socks, because sometimes his paperwork had coffee ring stains on it.

No…No…Then I remember (I have to force myself) it's because, on those same mornings, I am uncomfortable when he yells at other drivers, or me. It's because there have been nights when I've waited for him to come home with a newborn in my arms and he does not. It's because he is driving on some of those nights and I'm afraid that he will crash and fear drives me to drink myself just to calm myself down. It's because I've had to lock my bedroom door to keep him out. It's because I've smelled alcohol on his breath after he's been driving my daughter on the 101. It's because I've had to pick myself up out of my pneumonia-sick bed and pick them both up at a party because he was too drunk to drive them home. It's because I smell his breath sometimes when he comes to bed late and it smells like the bottom of a bar mat. Stale cigarettes and beer. Because she smells that too, and someday she will associate that smell with her wonderful loving daddy and wind up, herself, conflicted over the alcoholic whom she dearly loves but who may not be all he's cracked himself up to be.

Bubbling against this surface, those dark clouds are always there—threatening to appear and throw off our game. They are his actions and they are my fears and hesitations. I want to go shake him. If he would only change just one thing—just one. Then I wouldn't have to think these terrible thoughts of the destruction of our family. Then the ceiling would close and we could get back to playing the game well, on the same team and it would have the happy ending that my dad promised me I would have—once upon a time.

Denice

When I first met Greg his beautiful blue eyes were so full of life. He was brilliant, charming, handsome, athletic, motivated, and the life of the party. I was so happy our first year together. We had so much fun and he made me feel so loved. He made me feel alive.

But then he quit his job, started being moody, even angry and mean. He started not coming home at night, lying, and "borrowing" money regularly. He became mentally abusive. He told me that I embarrassed him, that none of our friends liked me, and that no one else would ever love me. I was so miserable and alone. I didn't understand what was happening. He convinced me I was going crazy and that everything was my fault. I hated myself for being so weak. What had happened to me? I had always been so strong and independent. I knew I should leave him, but I doubted myself and my sanity. I loved this man so much and he loved me. Why would I ever leave him? He was just "going through a phase". I just wanted the man I loved back.

I was about to lose my mind when Greg's stepfather told me the unthinkable. Greg was addicted to cocaine. I was absolutely dumbfounded. I was angry. I was sad. I felt so betrayed. I felt stupid. But I also felt relieved that maybe I wasn't the one who was crazy. At that point my nurturing instinct kicked in and I changed my focus to him. I had to help him and make him better. I couldn't give up on him, after all addiction is a disease. I was certain the love we had for each other would help him get better. He would do it for me, do it for us.

Greg went in and out of rehab and my life over the next nine months. Every so often he would disappear for several days at a time. I would be terrified thinking the worst, that he'd overdosed or been murdered. When I would cut him out of my life he would stalk me, call me up to fifty times a day, write me daily letters, break into my house, steal from me. My weak attempts at leaving him only caused me to hate myself even more when I would allow him back into my life. The sight of him mostly repulsed me but he had this power over me. I loved him more than I loved myself. He knew this and would use it to his advantage.

As time went by I started to let go, realizing life was passing me by and that I was allowing Greg's disease to ruin my life. But my guilt held me prisoner. I felt that I couldn t abandon the man that I loved and that he needed my support. That was until one day when I saw Greg differently. We had gone to a friend s out of town wedding. He disappeared for the entire night. I was humiliated, ashamed, and angry. But most of all I was done; I had finally hit my limit. The next day when I was checking out of the hotel alone, I saw him. I hardly recognized him. He had an arrogant grin on his face. His eyes looked possessed, black and beady, not blue, no life, just pure evil. That was when I realized he was no longer the man I had fallen in love with. I realized he loved that white powder way more than he ever loved me and that I was fighting a losing battle. I could never compete.

I left the hotel that day knowing that I had to move on and live my life. It took several months but I let go of Greg and his addiction, and started loving myself again. It was very difficult as I still loved him, but I finally loved myself more and stayed strong. My mind was made up. I wanted my life back and was ready to do whatever it took to achieve that.

First I moved 1000miles away. He followed me and started stalking me. I filed restraining orders. He came to my place of work and broke into my house repeatedly. I called the police and reported him many times. He continued to break in and even held me hostage one horrible Sunday morning. I sent him to jail. When his mother showed up to bail him out of jail I went to court to prevent his release. One might ask how did you endure all of this and remain strong and true to yourself? For the first time in my life I asked for help. I knew I would not be able to do it alone. I relied on friends and family who loved me, started seeing a counselor regularly, formed a relationship with the police department and the district attorney and did everything they suggested. It was a long difficult road but it was worth it. It is three years later and I am happy and healthy, have regained myself respect and confidence, am dating and enjoying life. I am once again the strong independent woman I used to be. I finally have myself and my life back.

Kristen

I am a double winner. My ex-husband and my son are both addicts. My ex-husband was always a heavy drinker but at some point became a full blown alcoholic. That ultimately ended our marriage, his relationship with our sons and his chance for any kind of a happy life. He has gone from being a husband, father and executive to being a homeless alcoholic. I tried everything I thought of to try and avoid this inevitable outcome but I didn't get one very important point. HE didn't want sobriety. This left my oldest son, who was 13, genetically predisposed and very angry, a bad combination. All the therapy , good and bad, did nothing to head off this impending train wreck. He started off slow with pot and over the course of 4 years turned into a garbage can addict and dealer.

I watched my son go down this road and again did everything I could to stop it, to change him. It didn't work, he was on a mission and he was good at it. The last year he was using was a nightmare for him, myself , and his little brother. I cried , grounded, pleaded, bribed, counseled, and then I cried and pleaded somemore. Eventually I watched him be taken to juvenille hall in handcuffs. Juvenille hall is close to our home and I drove by it so many times and wondered what it would be like to have a child go there, of course knowing that MY kids would never be there. Juvenille hall only served to pull him deeper into his addiction. I finally came to the realization when he was 17 that if I didn't do something drastic soon he would die!

I was able to send him to a treatment center in Utah for what ended up being over 7 months. He graduated after 6 months only to come home and relapse in a bad way(ER) within 1 week. He went back to Utah for 6 more weeks and this is when I knew something had to be different for all of us.

My younger son and I started going to alanon and alateen. One night at my alanon meeting a women came in and after listening to her talk I thought this is someone who knows stuff I didn't get yet, that was Carol. I had listened to everything at alanon about detaching and it sounded so painful and impossible because what they didn't help me with is how do I actually do that. Don't get me wrong alanon has been helpful and alateen has helped Riley alot. What I needed was the actual words to use and help following thru and keeping strong. I needed someone to walk me thru that step by step. The most painful part was that I knew I had to tell my son that he couldn't come home again. Carol helped do that in a loving way step by step. I can truly say that without her, or someone with her skills, I couldn't have done it. I needed her weekly support and guidance to get me thru it.

He has now been in sober living for 4 months and just moved out with sober friends and is doing better than I hoped for. He now knows he can't come back to our home town now. He has said "I know I wouldn't make it for more than 2 weeks without relapsing". He has found out how to have fun being sober. AA is a huge part of his life and he is very committed to his sobriety. I am so happy for him. We see each other often as he is only 1+ hours away. I know this is not the end of his journey. I also know that without the help I got we would not be at this place. Our relationship is on a completely different level. I don't watch over him and try to manage his life, he is learning to do that on his own. One thing he said to me that gives me comfort is " As long as I am sober I know everything will work out".

Traci

I remember feeling unbearably embarrassed and humiliated; wishing the ground would open up and swallow me.

That desperate, frantic panic left me in fight or flight mode. Who was I to fight? The love of my life? My soul mate?

There was no fighting the creature that he became once he really started drinking. He knew the consequences, what it did to me emotionally and psychologically. He thought he could stop whenever he wanted.

Why didn't he want to? Why did I believe he would?

I loved him too much to leave. I could feel my heart breaking every time I seriously considered it. After all, I was the only person who could avoid being in a situation that led to public humiliation.

I felt weak and frustrated. If he loved me, why couldn't he quit?

After realizing that his love for me had nothing to do with his disease, I didn't feel weak anymore. Despair started to take over. During a particularly difficult time of my life when I sincerely needed his support, he added to my burden and made my life significally more stressful.

Shortly after that, he began earnestly seeking sobriety. Something was different about this time; that endless black chasm of alcoholic hell stopped confronting me every day. Instead, my husband found a band of brothers and sisters who shared the struggle to stay out of the chasm together.

As he worked the twelve steps, he began to find interests again. He no longer thought of alcohol and its acquisition first thing. We have been enjoying sober living and the natural highs found every day.

I am still wary that my new life could slip back into the old ways, but I enjoy every day of his sobriety. Now, I feel like we are living instead of merely existing.

Elise

Troubles are often the tools by which God
fashions us for better things.

H. W. BEECHÀ

CONCLUSION

Well, here we are at the end, or is it the beginning? Yes, addiction can tear a family apart and often does. It will always linger in the background for the alcoholic / addict, the family, and the friends; that is just the nature of the disease. However, in the process of recovery, there is a significant opportunity to forge new and stronger ties between family members and friends.

If a marriage dissolves because the person addicted to alcohol or other drugs does not or cannot break free of those addictive chains, physically or emotionally, then so be it; though unfortunate and truly sad, you must move on to find a mate whose life is grounded and substance free. Try to remember that their behavior has had nothing to do with you. As the sage words from Al-Anon state, "You didn't cause it, you can't control it, and you can't cure it."

Our children, on the other hand, will always be our children and are a deep, dedicated part of our lives. I know that as frustrated, angry, and disappointed as I was that my daughter chose to embroil her teenage years in the world of drugs, I never lost hope, and I never stopped praying for her return to a comfortable, safe, and loving existence. However, sometimes parents have no choice but to finally let go of the frayed threads that bind them to their child when their child decides to continue a life of substance abuse. Please don't beat yourself up. Whether you personally believe in a higher power or not, take comfort in knowing that your child has a higher power of their own and that spiritual essence will guide them through their life.

My hope is that this book has given you some insight and tools for understanding and loving the alcoholic / addict in your life, as well as guiding you with empowering opportunities to become a stronger and more confident human being. Take action and trust yourself. You have no idea how smart and capable you really are!

Keep in mind the following key concepts as they will continue to help you reclaim your life with respect and dignity:

- Establish and stay true to your boundaries.
- Keep your expectations realistic.
- Stay neutral and refuse to engage.
- Don't take the bait.
- Enabling and rescuing are no longer options.
- Allow the alcoholic / addict to rebuild their life in their way.
- Make the recovery plan or contract bona fide and airtight between you and the alcoholic / addict.
- Find a passion that focuses on *your* life.

Be well; I applaud and respect your strength. Every person who reads this book is near and dear to me. We all travel the same path, shoulder to shoulder, right next door to each other or halfway around the world.

SEMINARS

One of my goals is to conduct a number of intense retreats for family members and friends to share their experiences, strengths, and hopes from the arsenal of ups and downs they accumulated while living their lives with the alcoholic/addict. In addition, role playing exercises depicting actual dialogue between the alcoholic/addict and the family member or friend are an excellent way to learn how to stay neutral and not engage. Cultivating strong communication skills, confident boundaries, and realistic expectations through lectures, case studies, and specific scenarios will round out a very educational weekend.

Please visit www.familyrecoverysolutions.com for more information, and if I can be of service, please don't hesitate to e-mail me.

NOTES

1 NCADD. "April 2010: 24th Annual NCADD Alcohol Awareness Month; When Love is Not Enough" (New York: NCADD, 2010)

2 Ibid.

3 Genetic Science Learning Center, Genetics is an Important Factor in Addiction, Learn.Genetics, 28 May 2010, http://learn.genetics.utah.edu/content/addiction/genetics/ (20 July 2010)

4 American Psychiatric Association. *Diagnostic and Statistical Manual of Mental Disorders, 4th Edition.* (Arlington, VA: American Psychiatric Publishing, Inc., 1994)

5 The A.A. General Service Conference-Approved Literature. "Is A.A. For You? Twelve Questions Only You Can Answer" (New York: Alcoholics Anonymous World Services, Inc., 2008)

6 *Al-Anon. Courage to Change: One Day at a Time in Al-Anon II.* (Virginia Beach, VA: Al-Anon Family Group Headquarters, Inc., 1992)

BIBLIOGRAPHY

Al-Anon Family Group. *Courage to Change: One Day at a Time in Al-Anon II.* Virginia Beach, VA: Al-Anon Family Group Headquarters, Inc., 1992.

Al-Anon Family Group. *One Day at a Time in Al-Anon.* Virginia Beach, VA: Al-Anon Family Group Headquarters, Inc., 1978.

Alcoholics Anonymous. The A.A. General Service Conference-approved literature. "Is A.A. for You? Twelve Questions Only You Can Answer" New York: Alcoholics Anonymous World Services, Inc., 2008.

American Psychiatric Association. *Diagnostic and Statistical Manual of Mental Disorders, 4th Edition.* Arlington, VA: American Psychiatric Publishing, Inc., 1994.

Canfield, Jack, and Hansen, Mark Victor. *Chicken Soup for the Soul.* Deerfield, FL: Health Communications, Inc., 1993.

Genetic Science Learning Center, University of Utah, http://learn.genetics.utah. edu. http://learn.genetics.utah.edu/content/addiction/genetics/

National Council on Alcoholism and Drug Dependence. "April 2010: 24th Annual NCADD Alcohol Awareness Month; When Love is Not Enough" promotional flyer. New York, New York: National Council on Alcoholism and Drug Dependence, Inc. (NCADD), 2010.

FILMOGRAPHY

Algren, Nelson (novel), Newman, Walter, Meltzer, Lewis. *The Man with the Golden Arm.* Directed by Otto Preminger. Otto Preminger, prod. United Artists, 1955.

Bass, Ronald, and Franken, Al. *When a Man Loves a Woman.* Directed by Jan Bananberg. Jon Avnet, prod. Touchstone Pictures, 1994.

Borchert, William G. and Thomasson, Camille. *When Love Is Note Enough: The Lois Wilson Story.* Directed by John Kent Harrison. Terry Gould, prod. Hallmark Hall of Fame, 2010.

Borchert, William G.*My Name is Bill W.* Directed by Daniel Petrie. Paul Rubell, prod. Warner Bros. Television, 1989.

Carroll, Tod. *Clean and Sober.* Directed by Glenn Gordon Caron. Ron Howard and Jay Daniel, prod. Warner Bros., 1988.

Cooper, Scott, and Cobb, Thomas (novel).*Crazy Heart.* Directed by Scott Cooper. Robert Duvall et. al., prod. Fox Searchlight Pictures, 2010.

Goluboff, Bryan (screenplay)Jim Carroll (novel). *The Basketball Diaries.* Directed by Scott Kalvert. Liz Heller and John Bard Manulis, prod. New Line Cinema, 1995.

Grant, Susannah. *28 Days.* Directed by Betty Thomas. Celia D. Costas, prod. Columbia Pictures, 2000.

Hamilton, Patrick, et. al. *Gaslight.* Directed by George Cukor. Arthur Hornblow Jr., prod. MGM, 1944.

Hixon, Ken. *City by the Sea.* Directed by Michael Caton-Jones. Don Carmody, Andrew Stevens, Roger Paradiso, and Dan Klores, prod. Warner Bros., 2002.

Lument, Jenny. *Rachel Getting Married.* Directed by Jonathan Demme. Jonathan Demme, Neda Armian, and Marc E. Platt, prod. Sony Pictures Classics, 2008.

Miller, JP. *The Days of Wine and Roses.*Directed by Blake Edwards. Martin Manulis, prod. Warner Bros., 1962.